Workshop on Cognitive Modeling and Computational Linguistics 2010

(CMCL 2010)

Held at ACL 2010

Uppsala, Sweden
15 July 2010

ISBN: 978-1-61738-812-5

Printed from e-media with permission by:

Curran Associates, Inc.
57 Morehouse Lane
Red Hook, NY 12571

Some format issues inherent in the e-media version may also appear in this print version.

Printed by Curran Associates, Inc. (2010)

For permission requests, please contact the Association for Computational Linguistics at the address below.

Association for Computational Linguistics
209 N. Eighth Street
Stroudsburg, Pennsylvania 18360

Phone: 1-570-476-8006
Fax: 1-570-476-0860

acl@aclweb.org

Additional copies of this publication are available from:

Curran Associates, Inc.
57 Morehouse Lane
Red Hook, NY 12571 USA
Phone: 845-758-0400
Fax: 845-758-2634
Email: curran@proceedings.com
Web: www.proceedings.com

Introduction

The papers in these proceedings were presented at the ACL-2010 workshop on *Cognitive Modeling and Computational Linguistics* held in Uppsala on July 15th 2010. The aim of the workshop was to provide a specialized venue for work in computational psycholinguistics. ACL Lifetime Achievement Award winner Martin Kay characterized this research area as striving to "build models of language that reflect in some interesting way on the ways in which people use language." The workshop continues a tradition of similar meetings held at the Cognitive Science Society annual meeting in 1997 and at ACL meetings in 1999 and 2004.

As organizer, I was happy to receive 23 submissions of which 10 were accepted. I would like to express my sincere thanks to the Program Committee for their help. Thank you — I look forward to seeing you at future CMCL workshops.

John T. Hale
July 2010

Organizer:

John T. Hale, Cornell University

Program Committee:

Steven Abney, University of Michigan
Matthew Crocker, Saarland University
Timothy O'Donnell, Harvard University
Michael C. Frank, MIT
Edward Gibson, MIT
Sharon Goldwater, University of Edinburgh
Keith Hall, Google
T. Florian Jaeger, University of Rochester
Mark Johnson, Macquarie University
Frank Keller, University of Edinburgh
Lars Konieczny, University of Freiburg
Roger Levy, UC San Diego
Rick Lewis, University of Michigan
Stephan Oepen, University of Oslo
Ulrike Padó, VICO Research & Consulting
David Reitter, Carnegie Mellon University
Brian Roark, Oregon Health & Science University
Doug Roland, University at Buffalo
Mats Rooth, Cornell University
William Schuler, Ohio State University
Richard Sproat, Oregon Health & Science University
Mark Steedman, University of Edinburgh
Patrick Sturt, University of Edinburgh
Sashank Varma, University of Minnesota
Shravan Vasishth, University of Potsdam
Amy Weinberg, University of Maryland

Table of Contents

Conference Program

Thursday July 15th 2010

Language change at multiple levels

9:00–9:30	*Using Sentence Type Information for Syntactic Category Acquisition* Stella Frank, Sharon Goldwater and Frank Keller
9:30–10:00	*Did Social Networks Shape Language Evolution? A Multi-Agent Cognitive Simulation* David Reitter and Christian Lebiere
10:00–10:30	*Syntactic Adaptation in Language Comprehension* Alex Fine, Ting Qian, T. Florian Jaeger and Robert Jacobs
10:30–11:00	Morning break

Parsing and memory

11:00–11:30	*HHMM Parsing with Limited Parallelism* Tim Miller and William Schuler
11:30–12:00	*The Role of Memory in Superiority Violation Gradience* Marisa Ferrara Boston
12:00–2:00	Lunch break

Corpus-based modeling

2:00–2:30	*Close = Relevant? The Role of Context in Efficient Language Production* Ting Qian and T. Florian Jaeger
2:30–3:00	*Predicting Cognitively Salient Modifiers of the Constitutive Parts of Concepts* Gerhard Kremer and Marco Baroni
3:00–3:30	*Towards a Data-Driven Model of Eye Movement Control in Reading* Mattias Nilsson and Joakim Nivre

Thursday July 15th 2010 (continued)

3:30–4:00	Afternoon break
	Information-theoretical approaches
4:00–4:30	*Modeling the Noun Phrase versus Sentence Coordination Ambiguity in Dutch: Evidence from Surprisal Theory* Harm Brouwer, Hartmut Fitz and John Hoeks
4:30–5:00	*Uncertainty Reduction as a Measure of Cognitive Processing Effort* Stefan Frank

Using Sentence Type Information for Syntactic Category Acquisition

Stella Frank (s.c.frank@sms.ed.ac.uk)
Sharon Goldwater (sgwater@inf.ed.ac.uk)
Frank Keller (keller@inf.ed.ac.uk)
School of Informatics, University of Edinburgh
10 Crichton Street, Edinburgh EH8 9AB, UK

Abstract

In this paper we investigate a new source of information for syntactic category acquisition: sentence type (question, declarative, imperative). Sentence type correlates strongly with intonation patterns in most languages; we hypothesize that these intonation patterns are a valuable signal to a language learner, indicating different syntactic patterns. To test this hypothesis, we train a Bayesian Hidden Markov Model (and variants) on child-directed speech. We first show that simply training a separate model for each sentence type decreases performance due to sparse data. As an alternative, we propose two new models based on the BHMM in which sentence type is an observed variable which influences either emission or transition probabilities. Both models outperform a standard BHMM on data from English, Cantonese, and Dutch. This suggests that sentence type information available from intonational cues may be helpful for syntactic acquisition cross-linguistically.

1 Introduction

Children acquiring the syntax of their native language have access to a large amount of contextual information. Acquisition happens on the basis of speech, and the acoustic signal carries rich prosodic and intonational information that children can exploit. A key task is to separate the acoustic properties of a word from the underlying sentence intonation. Infants become attuned to the pragmatic and discourse functions of utterances as signalled by intonation extremely early; in this they are helped by the fact that intonation contours of child and infant directed speech are especially well differentiated between sentence types (Stern et al., 1982; Fernald, 1989). Children learn to use appropriate intonational melodies to communicate their own intentions at the one word stage, before overt syntax develops (Snow and Balog, 2002).

It follows that sentence type information (whether a sentence is declarative, imperative, or a question), as signaled by intonation, is readily available to children by the time they start to acquire syntactic categories. Sentence type also has an effect on sentence structure in many languages (most notably on word order), so we hypothesise that sentence type is a useful cue for syntactic category learning. We test this hypothesis by incorporating sentence type information into an unsupervised model of part of speech tagging.

We are unaware of previous work investigating the usefulness of this kind of information for syntactic category acquisition. In other domains, intonation has been used to identify sentence types as a means of improving speech recognition language models. Specifically, (Taylor et al., 1998) found that using intonation to recognize dialogue acts (which to a significant extent correspond to sentence types) and then using a specialized language model for each type of dialogue act led to a significant decrease in word error rate.

In the remainder of this paper, we first present the Bayesian Hidden Markov Model (BHMM; Goldwater and Griffiths (2007)) that is used as the baseline model of category acquisition, as well as our extensions to the model, which incorporate sentence type information. We then discuss the distinctions in sentence type that we used and our evaluation measures, and finally our experimental results. We perform experiments on corpora in four different languages: English, Spanish, Cantonese, and Dutch. Our results on Spanish show no difference between the baseline and the models incorporating sentence type, possibly due to the small size of the Spanish corpus. Results on all other corpora show a small improvement in performance when sentence type is included as a cue to the learner. These cross-linguistic results suggest that sentence type may be a useful source of information to children acquiring syntactic categories.

2 BHMM Models

2.1 Standard BHMM

We use a Bayesian HMM (Goldwater and Griffiths, 2007) as our baseline model. Like a standard trigram HMM, the BHMM assumes that the probability of tag t_i depends only on the previous two tags, and the probability of word w_i depends only on t_i. This can be written as

$$t_i | t_{i-1} = t, t_{i-2} = t', \tau^{(t,t')} \sim \text{Mult}(\tau^{(t,t')}) \quad (1)$$

$$w_i | t_i = t, \omega^{(t)} \sim \text{Mult}(\omega^{(t)}) \quad (2)$$

where $\tau^{(t,t')}$ are the parameters of the multinomial distribution over following tags given previous tags (t, t')

Proceedings of the 2010 Workshop on Cognitive Modeling and Computational Linguistics, ACL 2010, pages 1–8,
Uppsala, Sweden, 15 July 2010.

and $\omega^{(t)}$ are the parameters of the distribution over outputs given tag t. The BHMM assumes that these parameters are in turn drawn from symmetric Dirichlet priors with parameters α and β, respectively:

$$\tau^{(t,t')}|\alpha \sim \text{Dirichlet}(\alpha) \quad (3)$$

$$\omega^{(t)}|\beta \sim \text{Dirichlet}(\beta) \quad (4)$$

Using these Dirichlet priors allows the multinomial distributions to be integrated out, leading to the following predictive distributions:

$$P(t_i|\mathbf{t}_{-i},\alpha) = \frac{C(t_{i-2},t_{i-1},t_i)+\alpha}{C(t_{i-2},t_{i-1})+T\alpha} \quad (5)$$

$$P(w_i|t_i,\mathbf{t}_{-i},\mathbf{w}_{-i},\beta) = \frac{C(t_i,w_i)+\beta}{C(t_i)+W_{t_i}\beta} \quad (6)$$

where $\mathbf{t}_{-i}=t_1\dots t_{i-1}$, $\mathbf{w}_{-i}=w_1\dots w_{i-1}$, $C(t_{i-2},t_{i-1},t_i)$ and $C(t_i,w_i)$ are the counts of the trigram (t_{i-2},t_{i-1},t_i) and the tag-word pair (t_i,w_i) in $\mathbf{t}_{-i}$ and $\mathbf{w}_{-i}$, T is the size of the tagset, and W_{t_i} is the number of word types emitted by t_i.

Based on these predictive distributions, (Goldwater and Griffiths, 2007) develop a Gibbs sampler for the model, which samples from the posterior distribution over tag sequences $\mathbf{t}$ given word sequences $\mathbf{w}$, i.e., $P(\mathbf{t}|\mathbf{w},\alpha,\beta)\propto P(\mathbf{w}|\mathbf{t},\beta)P(\mathbf{t}|\alpha)$. This is done by using Equations 5 and 6 to iteratively resample each tag t_i given the current values of all other tags.[1] The results show that the BHMM with Gibbs sampling performs better than the standard HMM using expectation-maximization. In particular, the Dirichlet priors in the BHMM constrain the model towards sparse solutions, i.e., solutions in which each tag emits a relatively small number of words, and in which a tag transitions to few following tags. This type of model constraint allows the model to find solutions which correspond to true syntactic parts of speech (which follow such a sparse, Zipfian distribution), unlike the uniformly-sized clusters found by standard maximum likelihood estimation using EM.

In the experiments reported below, we use the Gibbs sampler described by (Goldwater and Griffiths, 2007) for the BHMM, and modify it as necessary for our own extended models. We also follow (Goldwater and Griffiths, 2007) in using Metropolis-Hastings sampling for the hyperparameters, which are inferred automatically in all experiments. A separate β parameter is inferred for each tag.

2.2 BHMM with Sentence Types

We wish to add a sentence type feature to each time-step in the HMM, signalling the current sentence type. We treat sentence type (s) as an observed variable, on the assumption that it is observed via intonation or punctuation features (not part of our model), and these features are informative enough to reliably distinguish sentence types (as speech recognition tasks have found to be the case, see Section 1).

[1]Slight corrections need to be made to Equation 5 to account for sampling tags from the middle of the sequence rather than from the end; these are given in (Goldwater and Griffiths, 2007) and are followed in our own samplers.

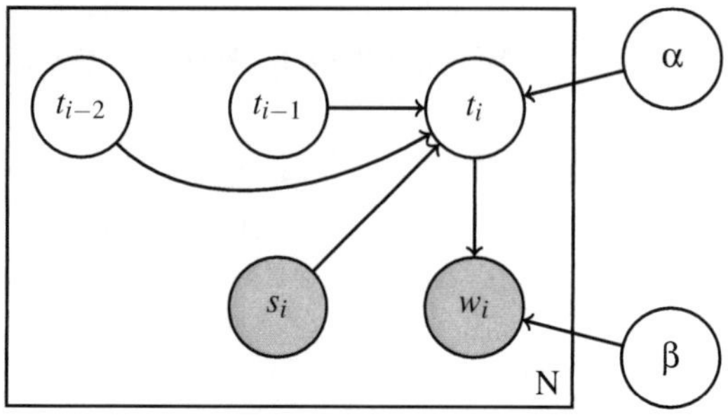

Figure 1: Graphical model representation of the BHMM-T, which includes sentence type as an observed variable on tag transitions (but not emissions).

In the BHMM, there are two obvious ways that sentence type could be incorporated into the generative model: either by affecting the transition probabilities or by affecting the emission probabilities. The first case can be modeled by adding s_i as a conditioning variable when choosing t_i, replacing line 1 from the BHMM definition with the following:

$$t_i|s_i=s,t_{i-1}=t,t_{i-2}=t',\tau^{(t,t')} \sim \text{Mult}(\tau^{(s,t,t')}) \quad (7)$$

We will refer to this model, illustrated graphically in Figure 1, as the BHMM-T. It assumes that the distribution over t_i depends not only on the previous two tags, but also on the sentence type, i.e., that different sentence types tend to have different sequences of tags.

In contrast, we can add s_i as a conditioning variable for w_i by replacing line 2 from the BHMM with

$$w_i|s_i=s,t_i=t,\omega^{(t)} \sim \text{Mult}(\omega^{(s,t)}) \quad (8)$$

This model, the BHMM-E, assumes that different sentence types tend to have different words emitted from the same tag.

The predictive distributions for these models are given in Equations 9 (BHMM-T) and 10 (BHMM-E):

$$P(t_i|t_{-i},s_i,\alpha)=\frac{C(t_{i-2},t_{i-1},t_i,s_i)+\alpha}{C(t_{i-2},t_{i-1},s_i)+T\alpha} \quad (9)$$

$$P(w_i|t_i,s_i,\beta)=\frac{C(t_i,w_i,s_i)+\beta}{C(t_i,s_i)+W_{t_i}\beta} \quad (10)$$

Of course, we can also create a third new model, the BHMM-B, in which sentence type is used to condition both transition and emission probabilities. This model is equivalent to training a separate BHMM on each type of sentence (with shared hyperparameters). Note that introducing the extra conditioning variable in these models has the consequence of splitting the counts for transitions, emissions, or both. The split distributions will therefore be estimated using less data, which could actually degrade performance if sentence type is not a useful variable.

Our prediction is that sentence type is more likely to be useful as a conditioning variable for transition probabilities (BHMM-T) than for emission probabilities (BHMM-E). For example, the auxiliary inversion in questions is likely to increase the probability of the AUX $\rightarrow$ PRO transition, compared to declaratives. Knowing that the sentence is a question may also affect emission probabilities, e.g., it might increase the probability the word *you* given a PRO and decrease the probability of *I*; one would certainly expect *wh*-words to have much higher probability in *wh*-questions than in declaratives. However, many other variables also affect the particular words used in a sentence (principally, the current semantic and pragmatic context). We expect that sentence type plays a relatively small role compared to these other factors. The ordering of tags within an utterance, on the other hand, is principally constrained by sentences type (especially in the short and grammatically simple utterances found in child-directed speech).

3 Sentence Types

We experiment with a number of sentence-type categories, leading to increasingly fine grained distinctions.

The primary distinction is between *questions* (Q) and *declaratives* (D). Questions are marked by punctuation (in writing) or by intonation (in speech), as well as by word order or other morpho-syntactic markers in many languages.

Questions may be separated into categories, most notably *wh-questions* and yes/no-questions. Many languages (including several English dialects) have distinct intonation patterns for *wh-* and yes/no-questions (Hirst and Cristo, 1998).

Imperatives are a separate type from declaratives, with distinct word order and intonation patterns.

Declaratives may be further subdivided into *fragments* and full sentences. We define fragments as utterances without a verb (including auxiliary verbs).

As an alternate sentence-level feature to sentence type, we use length. Utterances are classified according to their length, as either shorter or longer than average. Shorter utterances are more likely to be fragments and may have distinct syntactic patterns. However these patterns are likely to be less strong than in the above type-based types. In effect this condition is a pseudo-baseline, testing the effects of less- or non-informative sentence features on our proposed models.

4 Evaluation Measures

Evaluation of fully unsupervised part of speech tagging is known to be problematic, due to the fact that the part of speech clusters found by the model are unlabeled, and do not automatically correspond to any of the gold standard part of speech categories. We report three evaluation measures in our experiments, in order to avoid the weaknesses inherent in any single measure and in an effort to be comparable to previous work.

Matched accuracy (MA), also called many-to-one accuracy, is a commonly used measure for evaluating unlabeled clusterings in part of speech tagging. Each unlabeled cluster is given the label of the gold category with which it shares the most members. Given these labels, accuracy can be measured as usual, as the percentage of tokens correctly labeled. Note that multiple clusters may have the same label if several clusters match the same gold standard category. This can lead to a degenerate solution if the model is allowed an unbounded number of categories, in which each word is in a separate cluster. In less extreme cases, it makes comparing MA across clustering results with different numbers of clusters difficult. Another serious issue with MA is the "problem of matching" (Meila, 2007): matched accuracy only evaluates whether or not the items in the cluster match the majority class label. The non-matching items within a cluster might all be from a second gold class, or they might be from many different classes. Intuitively, the former clustering should be evaluated as better, but matched accuracy is the same for both clusterings.

Variation of Information (VI) (Meila, 2007) is a clustering evaluation measure that avoids the matching problem. It measures the amount of information lost and gained when moving between two clusterings. More precisely:

$$\begin{aligned} VI(C,K) &= H(C) + H(K) - 2I(C,K) \\ &= H(C|K) + H(K|C) \end{aligned}$$

A lower score implies closer clusterings, since each clustering has less information not shared with the other: two identical clusterings have a VI of zero. However, VI's upper bound is dependent on the maximum number of clusters in C or K, making it difficult to compare clustering results with different numbers of clusters.

As a third, and, in our view, most informative measure, we use *V-measure* (VM; Rosenberg and Hirschberg (2007)). Like VI, VM uses the conditional entropy of clusters and categories to evaluate clusterings. However, it also has the useful characteristic of being analogous to the precision and recall measures commonly used in NLP. Homogeneity, the precision analogue, is defined as

$$VH = 1 - \frac{H(C|K)}{H(C)}.$$

VH is highest when the distribution of categories within each cluster is highly skewed towards a small number of categories, such that the conditional entropy is low. Completeness (recall) is defined symmetrically to VH as:

$$VC = 1 - \frac{H(K|C)}{H(K)}.$$

VC measures the conditional entropy of the clusters within each gold standard category, and is highest if each category maps to a single cluster so that each

		Eve		Manchester	
Sentence type		Counts	$\|w\|$	Counts	$\|w\|$
	Total	13494	4.39	13216	4.23
D	Total	8994	4.48	8315	3.52
	I	623	4.87	757	4.22
	F	2996	1.73	4146	1.51
Q	Total	4500	4.22	4901	5.44
	wh	2105	4.02	1578	4.64
	Short utts	5684	1.89	6486	1.74
	Long utts	7810	6.21	6730	6.64

Table 1: Counts of sentence types in the Eve and Manchester training set. (Test and dev sets are approximately 10% of the size of training.) $|w|$ is the average length in words of utterances of this type. D: declaratives, I: imperatives, F: fragments, Q: questions, wh: *wh*-questions.

model cluster completely contains a category. The V-measure VM is simply the harmonic mean of VH and VC, analogous to traditional F-score. Unlike MA and VI, VM is invariant with regards to both the number of items in the dataset and to the number of clusters used, and consequently it is best suited for comparing results across different corpora.

5 English experiments

5.1 Corpora

We use the Eve corpus (Brown, 1973) and the Manchester corpus (Theakston et al., 2001) from the CHILDES collection (MacWhinney, 2000). The Eve corpus is a longitudinal study of a single US American child from the age of 1.5 to 2.25 years, whereas the Manchester corpus follows a cohort of 12 British children from the ages of 2 to 3. Using both corpora ensures that any effect is not due to a particular child, and is not specific to a type of English.

From both corpora we remove all utterances spoken by a child; the remaining utterances are nearly exclusively child-directed speech (CDS). We use the full Eve corpus and a similarly sized subset of the Manchester corpus, consisting of the first 70 CDS utterances from each file. Files from the chronological middle of each corpus are set aside for development and testing (Eve: file 10 for testing, 11 for dev; Manchester: file 17 from each child for testing, file 16 for dev).

Both corpora have been tagged using the relatively rich CHILDES tagset, which we collapse to a smaller set of thirteen tags: adjectives, adverbs, auxiliaries, conjunctions, determiners, infinitival-to, nouns, negation, participles, prepositions, pronouns, verbs and other (communicators, interjections, fillers and the like). *wh*-words are tagged as adverbs (*why*,*where*, *when* and *how*, or pronouns (*who* and the rest).

Table 1 show the sizes of the training sets, and the breakdown of sentence types within them. Each sentence type can be identified using a distinguishing characteristic. Sentence-final punctuation is used to differentiate between questions and declaratives; *wh*-questions are then further differentiated by the presence of a *wh*-word. Imperatives are separated from the declaratives by a heuristic (since CHILDES does not have an imperative verb tag): if an utterance includes a base verb within the first two words, without a pronoun proceeding it (with the exception of *you*, as in *you sit down right now*), the utterance is coded as an imperative. Fragments are also identified using the tag annotations, namely by the lack of a verb or auxiliary tag in an utterance.

The CHILDES annotation guide specifies that the question mark is to be used with any utterance with "final rising contour", even if syntactically the utterance might appear to be a declarative or exclamation. The question category consequently includes echo questions (*Finger stuck?*) and non-inverted questions (*You want me to have it?*).

5.2 Inference and Evaluation Procedure

Unsupervised models do not suffer from overfitting, so generally it is thought unnecessary to use separate training and testing data, with results being reported on the entire set of input data. However, there is still a danger, in the course of developing a model, of overfitting in the sense of becoming too finely attuned to a particular set of input data. To avoid this, we use separate test and development sets. The BHMM is trained on (train+dev) or (train+test), but evaluation scores are computed based on the dev or test portions of the data only. [2]

We run the Gibbs sampler for 2000 iterations, with hyperparameter resampling and simulated annealing. Each iteration produces an assignment of tags to the tokens in the corpus; the final iteration is used for evaluation purposes. Since Gibbs sampling is a stochastic algorithm, we run all models multiple times (three, except where stated otherwise) and report average values for all evaluation measures, as well as confidence intervals. We run our experiments using a variety of sentence type features, ranging from the coarse question/declarative (Q/D) distinction to the full five types. For reasons of space we do not report all results here, instead confining ourselves to representative samples.

5.3 BHMM-B: Type-specific Sub-Models

When separate sub-models are used for each sentence type, as in the BHMM-B, where both transition and emission probabilities are conditioned on sentence type, the hidden states (tags) in each sub-model do not correspond to each other, e.g., a hidden state 9 in one sub-model is not the same state 9 in another sub-model. Consequently, when evaluating the tagged output, each sentence type must be evaluated separately (otherwise the evaluation would equate declaratives-tag-9 with questions-tag-9).

[2] The results presented in this paper are all evaluated on the dev set; preliminary test set results on the Eve corpus show the same patterns.

Model	VM	VC	VH	VI	MA
wh-questions					
BHMM:	63.0 (1.0)	59.8 (0.4)	66.6 (1.8)	1.63 (0.03)	70.7 (2.7)
BHMM-B:	58.7 (2.0)	58.2 (2.1)	59.2 (2.0)	1.74 (0.09)	59.7 (2.0)
Other Questions					
BHMM:	65.6 (1.4)	62.7 (1.3)	68.7 (1.5)	1.62 (0.06)	74.5 (0.5)
BHMM-B:	64.4 (3.6)	62.6 (4.4)	66.2 (2.8)	1.65 (0.19)	70.8 (2.5)
Declaratives					
BHMM:	60.9 (1.3)	58.7 (1.1)	63.3 (1.6)	1.84 (0.06)	73.5 (0.8)
BHMM-B:	58.0 (1.2)	55.5 (1.1)	60.7 (1.5)	1.99 (0.06)	69.0 (1.5)

Table 2: Results for BHMM-B on W/Q/D sentence types (dev set evaluation) in the Manchester corpus, compared to the standard BHMM. The confidence interval is indicated in parentheses. Note that lower VI is better.

Model	VM	VC	VH	VI	MA
BHMM:	59.4 (0.2)	56.9 (0.2)	62.3 (0.2)	1.96 (0.01)	72.2 (0.2)
Q/D:	61.2 (1.2)	58.6 (1.2)	64.0 (1.4)	1.88 (0.06)	72.1 (1.5)
W/Q/D:	61.0 (1.7)	59.0 (1.5)	63.0 (2.0)	1.86 (0.08)	69.6 (2.2)
F/I/D/Q/W:	61.7 (1.7)	58.9 (1.8)	64.8 (1.6)	1.80 (0.09)	70.5 (1.3)

Table 3: Results for BHMM-E on the Eve corpus (dev set evaluation), compared to the standard BHMM. The confidence interval is indicated in parentheses.

Table 2 shows representative results for the W/Q/D condition on the Manchester corpus, separated into *wh*-questions, other questions, and declaratives. For each sentence type, the BHMM-B performs significantly worse than the BHMM. The *wh*-questions sub-model, which is trained on the smallest subset of the input corpus, performs the worst across all measures except VI. This suggests that lack of data is why these sub-models perform worse than the standard model.

5.4 BHMM-E: Type-specific Emissions

Having demonstrated that using entirely separate sub-models does not improve tagging performance, we turn to the BHMM-E, in which emission probability distributions are sentence-type specific, but transition probabilities are shared between all sentence types.

The results in Table 3 show that BHMM-E does result in slightly better tagging performance as evaluated by VI (lower VI is better) and VM and its components. Matched accuracy does not capture this same trend. Inspecting the clusters found by the model, we find that clusters for the most part do match gold categories. The tokens that do not fall into the highest matching gold categories are not distributed randomly, however; for instance, nouns and pronouns often end up in the same cluster. VI and VM capture these secondary matches while MA does not. Some small gold categories (e.g. the single word infinitival-*to* and negation-*not* categories) are often merged by the model into a single cluster, with the result that MA considers nearly half the cluster as misclassified.

The largest increase in performance with regards to the standard BHMM is obtained by adding the distinction between declaratives and questions. Thereafter, adding the *wh*-question, fragment and imperative sentence types does not worsen performance, but also does not significantly improve performance on any measure.

5.5 BHMM-T: Type-specific Transitions

Lastly, the BHMM-T shares emission probabilities among sentence types and uses sentence type specific transition probabilities.

Results comparing the standard BHMM with the BHMM-T with sentence-type-specific transition probabilities are presented in Table 4. Once again, VM and VI show a clear trend: the models using sentence type information outperform both the standard BHMM and models splitting according to utterance length (shorter/longer than average). MA shows no significant difference in performance between the different models (aside from clearly showing that utterance length is an unhelpful feature). The fact that the MA measure shows no clear change in performance is likely a fault of the measure itself; as explained above, VI and VM take into account the distribution of words within a category, which MA does not.

As with the BHMM-E, the improvements to VM and VI are obtained by distinguishing between questions and declaratives, and then between *wh*- and other questions. Both of these distinctions are marked by intonation in English. In contrast, distinguishing fragments and imperatives, which are less easily detected by intonation, provides no obvious benefit in any case. Using sentence length as a feature degrades performance considerably, confirming that improvements in performance are due to sentence types capturing useful information about the tagging task, and not simply due to splitting the input in some arbitrary way.

One reason for the improvement when adding the *wh*-question type is that the models are learning to identify and cluster the *wh*-words in particular. If we evaluate the *wh*-words separately, VM rises from 32.3

Model	VM	VC	VH	VI	MA
Eve					
BHMM:	59.4 (0.2)	56.9 (0.2)	62.3 (0.2)	1.96 (0.01)	72.2 (0.2)
Q/D:	60.9 (0.5)	58.3 (0.4)	63.7 (0.6)	1.89 (0.02)	72.7 (0.3)
W/Q/D:	**62.5** (1.2)	60.0 (1.3)	65.2 (1.0)	1.81 (0.06)	72.9 (0.8)
F/I/D/Q/W:	62.2 (1.5)	59.5 (1.6)	65.2 (1.3)	1.77 (0.08)	71.5 (1.4)
Length:	57.9 (1.2)	55.3 (1.1)	60.7 (1.3)	2.04 (0.06)	69.7 (2.0)
Manchester					
BHMM:	60.2 (0.9)	57.6 (0.9)	63.1 (1.0)	1.92 (0.05)	72.1 (0.7)
Q/D:	61.5 (0.7)	59.2 (0.6)	63.9 (0.9)	1.84 (0.03)	71.6 (1.5)
W/Q/D:	**62.7** (0.2)	60.6 (0.2)	65.0 (0.3)	1.78 (0.01)	71.2 (0.6)
F/I/D/Q/W:	62.5 (0.4)	60.3 (0.5)	64.9 (0.4)	1.79 (0.02)	71.3 (0.9)
Length:	58.1 (0.7)	55.6 (0.8)	60.8 (0.6)	2.02 (0.04)	71.0 (0.6)

Table 4: Results on the Eve and Manchester corpora for the various sentence types in the BHMM and BHMM-T models. The confidence interval is indicated in parentheses.

in the baseline BHMM to 41.5 in the W/Q/D condition with the BHMM-T model and 46.8 with the BHMM-E model. Performance for the non-*wh*-words also improves in the W/Q/D condition, albeit less dramatically: from 61.1 in the baseline BHMM to 63.6 with BHMM-T and 62.0 with BHMM-E. The *wh*-question type enables the models to pick up on the defining characteristics of these sentences, namely *wh*-words.

We predicted the sentence-type specific transition probabilities in the BHMM-T to be more useful than the sentence-type specific emission probabilities in the BHMM-E. The BHMM-T does perform slightly better than the BHMM-E, however, the effect is small. Word or tag order may be the most overt difference between questions and declaratives in English, but word choice, especially the use of *wh*-words varies sufficiently between sentence types for sentence-type specific emission probabilities to be equally useful.

6 Crosslinguistic Experiments

In the previous section we found that sentence type information improved syntactic categorisation in English. In this section, we evaluate the BHMM's performance on a range of languages other than English, and investigate whether sentence type information is useful across languages. To our knowledge this is the first application of the BHMM to non-English data.

Nearly all human languages distinguish between yes/no-questions and declaratives in intonation; questions are most commonly marked by rising intonation (Hirst and Cristo, 1998). *wh*-questions do not always have a distinct intonation type, but they are signalled by the presence of members of the small class of *wh*-words.

The CHILDES collection includes tagged corpora for Spanish and Cantonese: the Ornat corpus (Ornat, 1994) and the Lee Wong Leung (LWL) corpus (Lee et al., 1994) respectively. To cover a greater variety of word order patterns, a Dutch corpus of adult dialogue (not CDS) is also tested. We describe each corpus in turn below; Table 5 describes their relative sizes.

	Total	Ds	all Qs	*wh*-Qs
Spanish	8759	4825	3934	1507
$\|w\|$	4.29	4.41	4.14	3.72
Cantonese	12544	6689	5855	2287
$\|w\|$	4.16	3.85	4.52	4.80
Dutch	8967	7812	1155	363
$\|w\|$	6.16	6.19	6.00	7.08

Table 5: Counts of sentence types in the training sets for Spanish. Cantonese and Dutch. (Test and dev sets are approximately 10% of the size of training.) $|w|$ is the average length in words of utterances of this type. D: declaratives, Qs: questions, *wh*-Qs: *wh*-questions.

6.1 Spanish

The Ornat corpus is a longitudinal study of a single child between the ages of one and a half and nearly four years, consisting of 17 files. Files 08/09 are used testing/development.

We collapse the Spanish tagset used in the Ornat corpus in a similar fashion to the English corpora. There are 11 tags in the final set: adjectives, adverbs, conjuncts, determiners, nouns, prepositions, pronouns, relative pronouns, auxiliaries, verbs, and other.

Spanish *wh*-questions are formed by fronting the *wh*-word (but without the auxiliary verbs added in English); yes/no-questions involve raising the main verb (again without the auxiliary inversion in English). Spanish word order in declaratives is generally freer than English word order. Verb- and object-fronting is more common, and pronouns may be dropped (since verbs are marked for gender and number).

6.2 Cantonese

The LWL corpus consists of transcripts from a set of children followed over the course of a year, totalling 128 files. The ages of the children are not matched, but they range between one and three years old. Our training set consists of the first 500 utterances of all training files, in order to create a data set of similar size as the other corpora used. Files from children aged two years and five months are used as the test set; files from two years and six months are the development set files (again, the first 500 utterances from each of these make up the test/dev corpus).

The tagset used in the LWL is larger than the English corpus. It consists of 20 tags: adjective, adverb, aspectual marker, auxiliary or modal verb, classifier, communicator, connective, determiners, genitive marker, preposition or locative, noun, negation, pronouns, quantifiers, sentence final particle, verbs, wh-words, foreign word, and other. We remove all sentences that are encoded as being entirely in English but leave single foreign, mainly English, words (generally nouns) in a Cantonese context.

Cantonese follows the same basic SVO word order as English, but with a much higher frequency of topic-raising. Questions are not marked by different word order. Instead, particles are inserted to signal questioning. These particles can signal either a yes/no-question or a *wh*-question; in the case of *wh*-questions they replace the item being questioned (e.g., *playing-you what?*), without *wh*-raising as in English or Spanish. Despite the use of tones in Cantonese, questions are marked with rising final intonation.

6.3 Dutch

The Corpus of Spoken Dutch (CGN) contains Dutch spoken in a variety of settings. We use the "spontaneous conversation" component, consisting of 925 files, since it is the most similar to CDS. However, the utterances are longer, and there are far fewer questions, especially *wh*-questions (see Table 5).

The corpus does not have any meaningful timeline, so we designated all files with numbers ending in 0 as test files and files ending in 9 as dev files. The first 60 utterances from each file were used, to create training/test/dev sets similar in size to the other corpora.

The coarse CGN tagset consists of 11 tags, which we used directly: adjective, adverb, conjunction, determiner, interjection, noun, number, pronoun/determiner, preposition, and verb.

Dutch follows verb-second word order in main clauses and SOV word order in embedded clauses. Yes/no-questions are created by verb-fronting, as in Spanish. *wh*-questions involve a *wh*-word at the beginning of the utterance followed by the verb in second position.

6.4 Results

We trained standard BHMM, BHMM-T and BHMM-E models in the same manner as with the English corpora. Given the poor performance of the BHMM-B, we did not test it here.

Due to inconsistent annotation and lack of familiarity with the languages we tested only two sentence type distinctions, Q/D and W/Q/D. Punctuation was used to distinguish between questions and declaratives. *wh*-questions were identified by using a list of *wh*-words for Spanish and Dutch; for Cantonese we relied on the *wh*-word tag annotation.

Results are shown in Table 6. Since the corpora are different sizes and use tagsets of varying sizes, VI and MA results are not comparable between corpora. VM (and VC and VH) are more robust, but even so cross-corpora comparisons should be made carefully. The English corpora VM scores are significantly higher (around 10 points higher) than the non-English corpora scores.

In Cantonese and Dutch, the W/Q/D BHMM-T model performs best; in both cases significantly better than the BHMM. In Cantonese, the separation of *wh*-questions improves tagging significantly in both the BHMM-T and BHMM-E models, whereas simply separating questions and declaratives helps far less. In the Dutch corpus, *wh*-questions improved only in the BHMM-T, not in the BHMM-E.

The Spanish models have higher variance, due to the small size of the corpus. Due to the high variance, there are no significant differences between any of the conditions; it is also difficult to spot a trend.

7 Future Work

We have shown sentence type information to be useful for syntactic tagging. However, the BHMM-E and BHMM-T models are successful in part however because they also share information as well as split it; the completely split BHMM-B does not perform well. Many aspects of tagging do not change significantly between sentence types. Within a noun phrase, the ordering of determiners and nouns is the same whether it is in a question or an imperative, and to a large extent the determiners and nouns used will be the same as well. Learning these patterns over as much input as possible is essential. Therefore, the next step in this line of work will be to add a general (corpus-level) model alongside type-specific models. Ideally, the model will learn when to use the type-specific model (when tagging the beginning of questions, for instance) and when to use the general model (when tagging NPs). Such a model would make use of sentence-type information in a better way, hopefully leading to further improvements in performance. A further, more sophisticated model could learn the useful sentence types distinctions automatically, perhaps forgoing the poorly performing imperative or fragment types we tested here in favor of a more useful type we did not identify.

8 Conclusions

We set out to investigate a hitherto unused source of information for models of syntactic category learning, namely intonation and its correlate, sentence type. We showed that this information is in fact useful, and including it in a Bayesian Hidden Markov Model improved unsupervised tagging performance.

We found tagging performance increases if sentence type information is used to generate either transition probabilities or emission probabilities in the BHMM. However, we found that performance decreases if sentence type information is used to generate both transi-

Model	VM	VC	VH	VI	MA
Spanish					
BHMM:	49.4 (1.8)	47.2 (1.9)	51.8 (1.8)	2.27 (0.09)	61.5 (2.1)
BHMM-E Q/D:	49.4 (1.5)	47.0 (1.4)	52.1 (1.7)	2.28 (0.06)	60.9 (2.6)
BHMM-E W/Q/D:	48.7 (2.5)	46.4 (2.4)	51.2 (2.6)	2.31 (0.11)	60.2 (3.0)
BHMM-T Q/D:	49.0 (1.7)	46.7 (1.6)	51.6 (1.7)	2.30 (0.07)	60.9 (2.5)
BHMM-T W/Q/D:	49.5 (2.5)	47.2 (2.3)	52.1 (2.8)	2.27 (0.11)	61.0 (3.0)
Cantonese					
BHMM:	49.4 (0.8)	44.5 (0.7)	55.4 (1.0)	2.60 (0.04)	67.2 (1.0)
BHMM-E Q/D:	50.7 (1.6)	45.4 (1.5)	57.5 (1.7)	2.55 (0.09)	69.0 (1.0)
BHMM-E W/Q/D:	**52.3** (0.3)	46.9 (0.3)	59.3 (0.4)	2.46 (0.02)	69.4 (0.9)
BHMM-T Q/D:	50.3 (0.9)	45.0 (0.9)	57.0 (1.0)	2.57 (0.05)	68.4 (0.8)
BHMM-T W/Q/D:	**52.2** (0.8)	46.8 (0.9)	59.1 (0.7)	2.47 (0.05)	69.9 (1.9)
Dutch					
BHMM:	48.4 (0.7)	47.1 (0.8)	49.7 (0.7)	2.38 (0.04)	62.3 (0.3)
BHMM-E Q/D:	48.4 (0.4)	47.3 (0.4)	49.7 (0.5)	2.37 (0.02)	62.2 (0.3)
BHMM-E W/Q/D	47.6 (0.3)	46.3 (0.4)	48.8 (0.2)	2.41 (0.02)	61.2 (1.1)
BHMM-T Q/D:	47.9 (0.5)	46.7 (0.4)	49.1 (0.5)	2.40 (0.02)	61.5 (0.4)
BHMM-T W/Q/D:	**49.6** (0.2)	48.5 (0.2)	50.8 (0.2)	2.31 (0.10)	64.1 (0.2)

Table 6: Results for BHMM, BHMM-E, and BHMM-T on non-English corpora.

tion and emission probabilities (which is equivalent to training a separate BHMM for each sentence type).

To test the generality of our findings, we carried out a series of cross-linguistic experiments, integrating sentence type information in unsupervised tagging models for Spanish, Cantonese, and Dutch. The results for Cantonese and Dutch mirrored those for English, showing a small increase in tagging performance for models that included sentence type information. For Spanish, no improvement was observed.

References

Roger Brown. 1973. *A first language: The early stages*. Harvard University Press.

Anne Fernald. 1989. Intonation and communicative intent in mothers' speech to infants: Is the melody the message? *Child Development*, 60(6):1497–1510.

Sharon Goldwater and Thomas L. Griffiths. 2007. A fully Bayesian approach to unsupervised part-of-speech tagging. In *Proceedings of the 45th Annual Meeting of the Association of Computational Linguistics*.

Daniel Hirst and Albert Di Cristo, editors. 1998. *Intonation systems: a survey of twenty languages*. Cambridge University Press.

Thomas H.T. Lee, Colleen H Wong, Samuel Leung, Patricia Man, Alice Cheung, Kitty Szeto, and Cathy S P Wong. 1994. The development of grammatical competence in cantonese-speaking children. Technical report, Report of RGC earmarked grant 1991-94.

Brian MacWhinney. 2000. *The CHILDES Project: Tools for Analyzing Talk*. Lawrence Erlbaum Associates, Mahwah, NJ.

Marina Meila. 2007. Comparing clusterings – an information based distance. *Journal of Multivariate Analysis*, 98:873–895.

Susana Lopez Ornat. 1994. *La adquisicion de la lengua espagnola*. Siglo XXI, Madrid.

Andrew Rosenberg and Julia Hirschberg. 2007. V-measure: A conditional entropy-based external cluster evaluation measure. In *EMNLP*.

David Snow and Heather Balog. 2002. Do children produce the melody before the words? A review of developmental intonation research. *Lingua*, 112:1025–1058.

Daniel N. Stern, Susan Spieker, and Kristine MacKain. 1982. Intonation contours as signals in maternal speech to prelinguistic infants. *Developmental Psychology*, 18(5):727–735.

Paul A. Taylor, S. King, S. D. Isard, and H. Wright. 1998. Intonation and dialogue context as constraints for speech recognition. *Language and Speech*, 41(3):493–512.

Anna Theakston, Elena Lieven, Julian M. Pine, and Caroline F. Rowland. 2001. The role of performance limitations in the acquisition of verb-argument structure: an alternative account. *Journal of Child Language*, 28:127–152.

Did Social Networks Shape Language Evolution?
A Multi-Agent Cognitive Simulation

David Reitter
Department of Psychology
Carnegie Mellon University
Pittsburgh, PA, USA
reitter@cmu.edu

Christian Lebiere
Department of Psychology
Carnegie Mellon University
Pittsburgh, PA, USA
cl@cmu.edu

Abstract

Natural language as well as other communication forms are constrained by cognitive function and evolved through a social process. Here, we examine whether human memory may be uniquely adapted to the social structures prevalent in groups, specifically small-world networks. The emergence of domain languages is simulated using an empirically evaluated ACT-R-based cognitive model of agents in a naming game played within communities. Several community structures are examined (grids, trees, random graphs and small-world networks). We present preliminary results from small-scale simulations, showing relative robustness of cognitive models to network structure.

1 Introduction

A language, even if shared among the members of a community, is hardly static. It is constantly evolving and adapting to the needs of its speakers. Adaptivity in natural language has been found at various linguistic levels. Models of *dialogue* describe how interlocutors develop representation systems in order to communicate; such systems can, for instance, be observed using referring expressions such as *the wall straight ahead* that identify locations in a maze. Experiments have shown that communities converge on a common standard for such expressions (Garrod and Doherty, 1994).

Models of the horizontal *transmission of cultural information* within generations show on a much larger scale how beliefs or communicative standards spread within a single generation of humans. Recently, language change has accelerated through the use of communication technologies, achieving changes that used to take generations in years or even months or weeks. However, the structure of electronic networks mimics that of more traditional social networks, and even communication via mass media follows a power-law-driven network topology.

The individual agents that are effecting the language change depend on their cognitive abilities such as memory retrieval and language processing to control and accept novel communication standards. Do the local, cognitive constraints at the individual level interact with the structure of large-scale networks? Both social structure and individual cognitive systems have evolved over a long period of time, leading to the hypothesis that certain network structures are more suitable than others to convergence, given the specific human cognitive apparatus. Some properties of human cognition are well established, e.g., in cognitive frameworks (Anderson et al., 2004). Was human cognition shaped by social networks? Why are memory parameters the way they are? Social network structures may hold an answer to this question. If so, we should find that naturally occurring networks structures are uniquely suited to human learning, while others will perform less well when human learners are present.

The environment may have been influenced by individual cognition as well. Why are social networks structured the way they are? Human memory and possibly human learning strategies are the result of an evolutionary process. Social network structures can be explained by models such as *Preferential Attachment* (Barabasi and Albert, 1999), yet, even that is tied to evolved distributions of preferences in human agents. Dall'Asta et al. (2006) argue that the dynamic of agreement in small-world networks shows, at times, properties that ease the (cognitive) memory burden on the individuals. It is possible that the human memory apparatus and social preferences governing network structures have co-evolved. Such a theory would, again, suggest the hypothesis underly-

Proceedings of the 2010 Workshop on Cognitive Modeling and Computational Linguistics, ACL 2010, pages 9–17,
Uppsala, Sweden, 15 July 2010.

ing this study: that network structure and human memory are co-dependent.

2 Modeling Language Change

Network structure, on a small scale, does influence the evolving patterns of communication. The dichotomy between individual and community-based learning motivated experiments by Garrod et al. (2007) and Fay et al. (2010), where participants played the *Pictionary* game. In each trial of this naming game, each participant is paired up with another participant. One of them is then to make a drawing to convey a given concept out of a small set of known concepts; the other one is to select the concept from that list without engaging in verbal communication. Over time, participants develop common standards codifying those concepts: they develop a system of meaning-symbol pairs, or, *signs*. We take this system as the lexical core of the shared language. The convergence rate and the actual language developed differed as a function of the structure of the small participant communities: Fay (2010) either asked the same pairs of participants to engage in the activity repeatedly, or matched up different pairs of participants over time. Fay and Garrod's Pictionary experiments served as the empirical basis for a cognitive process model developed by (Reitter and Lebiere, 2009). Our model has agents propose signs by combining more elementary signs from their divergent knowledge bases, and also adopt other agent's proposals of signs for later reuse. The model, designed to match Fay's communities, was studied in a condition involving groups of eight agents, with two network structures: maximally disjoint with the same pairs of agents throughout the simulation, and maximally connected, with interactions between all possible pairs of agents.

Reitter and Lebiere's (2009) cognitive model reflects the Pictionary game. The model explains the convergence as a result of basic learning and memory retrieval processes, which have been well understood and made available for simulation in a cognitive modeling framework, ACT-R Anderson et al. (2004). Thus, properties of human memory and of the agent's learning strategies dictate how quickly they adopt signs or establish new signs: processes such as learning, forgetting and noise together with their fundamental parameters that are within well-established ranges provide strong constraints on the behavior of each agent and in turn the evolution of their communication within the network. This approach acknowledges that cultural evolution is constrained by individual learning; each agent learns according to their cognitive faculty (cf., Christiansen and Chater, 2008). With non-cognitive models, language change has been simulated on a larger scale as well (e.g., Kirby and Hurford, 2002; Brighton et al., 2005).

It is because adaptation according to experience is determined by human learning behavior that simulation in validated learning frameworks is crucial. Griffiths and Kalish (2007) for instance model language evolution through iteration among rational learners in a Bayesian framework; the purpose of the present project is to tie the simulation of language evolution to a concrete experiment and a more process-oriented cognitive architecture than the Bayesian framework. *ACT-R*'s learning mechanisms extend the Bayesian view with at least a notion of recency. Work on language processing has pointed out its relationship to memory retrieval from within the ACT-R framework, both for language comprehension (Budiu and Anderson, 2002; Lewis and Vasishth, 2005; Crescentini and Stocco, 2005; Ball et al., 2007) and for language production (Reitter, 2008). The individual language faculty as a result of biological evolution and adaptation to cultural language has been the focus of psycholinguistic models proposing specialized mechanisms (the Chomskian viewpoint); our model does not propose a specialized mechanism but rather declarative memory as store for lexical information, and procedural cognitive processes as regulators of certain communicative functions. Our multi-agent model sees part of the linguistic process as an instantiation of general cognition: the composition and retrieval of signs follows general cognitive mechanisms and can be formulated within cognitive frameworks such as ACT-R (Anderson et al., 2004) or SOAR (Laird and Rosenbloom, 1987).

In this study, we adapted the 2009 model and simulated language convergence in several larger-scale networks. We investigate the relationship between human memory function in the retrieval of linguistic items and the structure of social networks on which humans depend to communicate.

3 Network structures

Differences in naturally occurring social networks are hardly as extreme as in Fay's experiment. Some agents will be connected to a large number of other ones, while many agents will have just a few connections each. Concretely, the number of interaction partners of a randomly chosen community member is not normally distributed and centered around a mean. It shows a (Zipfian) power law distribution, with a number of hubs attracting many network neighbors, and a long tail of subjects interacting with just a few other ones each. Social networks are *small world* networks: the average distance between any two nodes in the networks is low, since many of them are connected to hubs. Non-organically connected communication and command networks follow other normals–tree graphs for instance. However, natural communication standards develop in networks that have very specific properties that can be observed in most organically developed networks.

Realistic social networks commonly show very specific properties. Social networks, in which links symbolize communication pathways or some form of social acquaintance, frequently exhibit the *small world* property. The mean minimum distance between any two nodes is relatively low, and the clustering coefficient is high (Watts and Strogatz, 1998).

Other forms of networks include tree hierarchies with a constant or variable branching factor (directed acyclic graphs). Such networks ressemble communication and command hierarchies in military or business organizations. N-dimensional grid networks have nodes with constant degrees, which are connected to each of their two neighbors along each dimension in a lattice.

Much work on information or belief propagation, or decision-making in networks has used large artificial networks modeled after social ones; nodes in such networks are commonly simple agents that make decisions based on input fed to them by their neighbor nodes and pass on information. These often state-less agents do not necessarily employ learning or adaptivity, and when they do, learning does not reflect known cognitive properties of human memory. The mechanisms governing learning and retrieval in human memory have been studied in detail, leading to formal models of process that detail the units that may be stored in and retrieved from memory, the retrieval time and accuracy depending on the frequency and recency of prior rehearsals, on contextual cues that may facilitate retrieval, and on individual differences. Cognitive agents can serve as a more realistic basis for network simulations (Sun, 2001).

Frequency, recency, contextual cues and chunking of the stored information determine retrieval probability, which is crucial when novel idioms are required to express meaning in communication. The process leads to the choice of one of several available synonyms. Our model sees this decision-making process as a matter of memory retrieval: given the desired meaning, which sign (word or drawing, compound noun or drawings) can be used to express it. This process is implicit (not consciously controlled), and it follows recent suggestions from cognitive psychology: Pickering and Garrod's (2004) Interactive Alignment Model proposes that explicit negotiation and separate models of the interlocutor's mental state aren't necessary, as long as each speaker is coherent and adapts to their interlocutors, as speakers are known to do on even simple, linguistic levels (lexical, syntactic). This shifts the weight of the task from a sophisticated reasoning device to the simpler, more constrained implicit learning mechanism of the individual.

The social network controls the interactions that the agents can experience. Each interaction is an opportunity to develop new signs and adapt the existing communication systems. It can be shown that even separate pairs of agents develop specialized communication systems, both empirically (Garrod and Doherty, 1994; Reitter and Moore, 2007; Kirby and Hurford, 2002) and in the specific model used here.When communication partners change, convergence towards a common system and the final transmission accuracy is slower (Fay et al., 2008). At this point it is unclear how the structure of the communication network and the learning process interact. Given that some types of networks show a wide distribution of degrees, where some nodes communicate much more often and with a wide variety of neighbors, while others communicate less often, recency and frequency of memory access will vary substantially. Other communication networks may reflect command hierarchies in organizations, which are constructed to ensure, among other things, more predictable information propagation.

We hypothesize that the human memory apparatus and preferred social network structures have co-evolved to be uniquely suited to create a macro-organism that adapts its communication structures and reasoning mechanisms to novel situations. There is limited opportunity to test such a hypothesis under controlled conditions with a sufficiently large human network; however, cognitive models that have been developed to explain and predict human performance in isolated cognitive situations can be leveraged to study the development of sign systems.

In a simulated network with cognitive models representing agents at the network nodes, and communication between agents along network links, we expect that the social network structures lead to better, if not optimal, adaptivity during the establishment of a communication system. We expect that scale-free small world networks do best, outperforming tree hierarchies, random networks and regular grids (lattices).

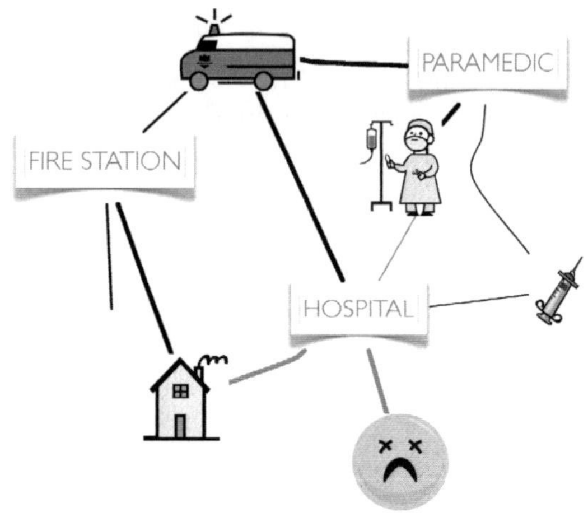

Figure 1: Example of a small ontology with abstract concepts (spelled-out words) and concrete ones (drawings).

3.1 Architecture

ACT-R's memory associates symbolic chunks of information (sets of feature-value pairs) with subsymbolic, activation values. Learning occurs through the creation of such a chunk, which is then reinforced through repeated presentation, and forgotten through decay over time. The symbolic information stored in chunks is available for explicit reasoning, while the subsymbolic information moderates retrieval, both in speed and in retrieval probability. The assumption of rationality in ACT-R implies that retrievability is governed by the expectation to make use of a piece of information at a later point. Important to our application, retrieval is further aided by contextual cues. When other chunks are in use (e.g., *parliament*), they support the retrieval of related chunks (*building*).

The properties of memory retrieval in terms of time and of retrieval success are governed by the *activation* of a chunk that is to be retrieved. Three components of activation are crucial in the context of this model: *base-level activation*, *spreading activation* and *transient noise* (ϵ). Base-level activation is predictive of retrieval probability independent of the concurrent context. It is determined by the frequency and recency of use of the particular chunk, with t_j indicating the time elapsed since use k of the chunk. d indicates a base-level decay parameter, usually 0.5):

$$A_i = \log \sum_{k=1}^{pres} t_k^{-d} + \sum_{j}^{cues} w_j S_{ji} + \epsilon$$

Retrieval is contextualized by cues available through spreading activation. It is proportional to the strengths of association (S_{ji}) of all of the cues with the target chunk. While the base-level term (first term of the sum) can be seen as a prior, spreading activation models the conditional probability of retrieval given the available cues. Finally, ϵ is sampled from a logistic distribution shaped by canonical parameters. A_i must surpass a minimum *retrieval threshold*.

The model is implemented using the ACT-UP toolbox, which makes the components of the ACT-R theory are directly accessible. The cognitive model does not specify other model components (perceptual, manual, procedural), as they are neither subject to evaluation nor considered to make a significant contribution to learning or convergence effects.

3.2 Communication model

We assume that the communication system, or *language*, is a *system of signs*. Concretely, it is a set of tuples (*signs*), each associating a *meaning* with a set of up to three *symbols* (a simplifying assumption). If the communication system uses natural language, symbols consist of spoken or written words. The communication system established by the participants of Garrod's and Fay's experiments uses drawings as symbols–the principle stays the same. Agents start out with a knowledge base containing signs for concrete concepts that are immediately representable as drawings or nouns; the target concepts to be conveyed by the participants, however, are more abstract and require the combination of such concrete concepts. A concept such as *hospital*, for instance, could involve the drawings for *house*, *ambulance*, and a *sad face*. A participant could choose among many ways to express *hospital*.

The goal of our cognitive models is to communicate meaning from one agent to another one. Put in natural language-oriented terminology, the *director* role is the *speaker*, a role that involves selecting the right concrete concepts that can express a given target concepts; the *matcher* role (*listener*) involves decoding the concrete drawings (or words) to retrieve the target.

A single ACT-R model implements the *director* and *matcher* roles. As a director, the model establishes new combinations of drawings for given target concepts. As a matcher, the model makes guesses. In each role, the model revises its internal mappings between drawings and target concepts. The model is copied to instantiate a community of agents, one for each node in the network.

The simplest form of representing a communication system in ACT-R memory *chunks* is as a set of signs. Each sign pairs a concept with a set of drawings. Competing signs can be used to assign multiple drawings for one conceptTo reflect semantic relationships, we need to introduce a subsymbolic notion of relatedness. We use ACT-R's spreading activation mechanism and weights between concepts to reflect relatedness. Spreading activation facilitates retrieval of a chunk if the current context offers cues related to the chunk. Relatedness is expressed as a value in log-odds space (S_{ji} *values*).

When the model is faced with the task to draw a given concept such as *Russell Crowe* (one of the concepts in the experiment) or *Hospital* (as in Figure 1) that has no canonical form as a drawing, a related but concrete concept is retrieved from declarative memory (such as Syringe in the example). In drawing-based communication, this would be a concept that can be drawn, while in natural-language based communication, this is an existing drawing expressing a similar, partial or otherwise related concept. We request two other such concepts, reflecting the desire of the communicator to come up with a distinctive rather than just fitting depiction of the target concept. The case of a model recognizing a novel combination of drawings is similar; we retrieve the concept using the drawings as cues that spread activation, making the target concept the one that is the most related one to the drawings.

After drawings have been produced or recognized and mapped to a target, the target or guessed concept, along with the component drawings, is stored symbolically in memory as a chunk for later reuse (*domain sign*). These signs differ from the pre-existing concepts in the network, although they also allow for the retrieval of suitable drawings given a concept, and for a concept given some drawings. When drawing or recognizing at a later stage, the memorized domain signs are strictly preferred as a strategy over the retrieval of related concepts. The system of domain signs encodes what is agreed upon as a language system between two communicators; they will be reused readily during drawing when interacting with a new partner, but they will be of only limited use when attempting to recognize a drawing combination that adheres to somebody else's independently developed communication system.

Thus, the model has two avenues to express and recognize an abstract concept: by associative retrieval and by idiomatic domain concept. A message constructed by domain concept retrieval is often decoded by the matcher by association, and vice versa.

The identification accuracy of the model shows characteristics observed in empirical work (Fay et al. 2008). See Reitter and Lebiere (subm) for a detailed description of the model and its evaluation.

3.3 Knowledge

Agents start out with shared world knowledge. This is expressed as a network of concepts, connected by weighted links (S_{ji}). The distribution of link strengths is important in this context, as it determines how easily we can find drawing combinations that reliably express target concepts. Thus, the S_{ji} were sampled randomly from an empirical distribution: log-odds derived from the frequencies of collocations found in text corpus data. From the *Wall Street Journal* corpus we extracted and counted pairs of nouns that co-occurred in the same sentence (e.g., "market", "plunge"). As ex-

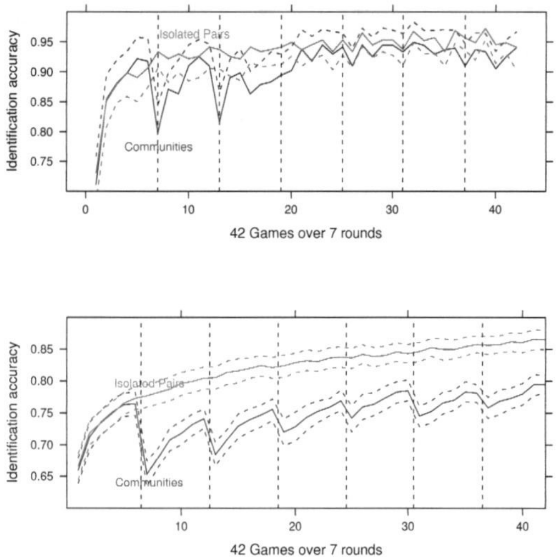

Figure 2: Identification accuracy for isolated pairs and communities: (a) human data as provided by Fay (p.c.), (b) simulation. One-tailed standard-error based 95% confidence intervals (upper bounds for communities, lower bounds for pairs) for human data; two-tailed 95% via bootstrapping for simulations. As in the human data, both community pairs and isolated pairs converge most in the early rounds, but community pairs lose much accuracy when switching partners.

pected, the frequencies of such collocations are distributed according to a power law.

Such knowledge is, however, not fully shared between agents. Each agent has their own knowledge network resulting from life experience. This difference is essential to the difficulty of the task: if all agents came to the same conclusions about the strongest representation of target concepts, there would be little need to establish the domain language. We control the noise applied to the link strengths between concepts j and i for agent M (S^M_{ji}) by combining the common ground S_{ji} (shared between all agents) with a random sample N^M_{ji} in a mixture model: $S^M_{ji} = (1-n)S_{ji} + nN^M_{ji}$; sign identification accuracy was found to be stable for n up to about 0.4; we set it to 0.3 for Simulation 1.

4 Simulation 1

Networks of individual cognitive agents were created to differentiate performance between four different network structures. **Random networks** contain N nodes with randomly assigned links between them, on average d links for each node (Erdős and Rényi, 1959). n-dimensional **Grids** contain N nodes with a constant numer of links d per node, with links between neighbors along each dimension. The width w is kept the same along each dimension, i.e. there are w nodes per row. We use 6-dimensional lattices. **Trees** are directed acyclic graphs with 1 link leading up, and $d-1$ links (branching factor) leading down the hierarchy of a total of N nodes. **Scale-free networks** are constructed using the *preferential attachment* method as follows (Barabasi and Albert, 1999). N nodes are created and each is connected to one randomly selected other node. Then, two links $< a, b >$ and $< a', b' >$ are chosen randomly out of the existing set of links, and a new link $< a, b' >$ is added, until the mean degree d (links per node) is reached. Preferential attachment ensures that nodes with a high number of links acquire further links more quickly than other nodes (*the rich get richer*). This yields a power-law distribution of degrees. Our scale-free networks display small world properties.

For the first Simulation, we control N at 85 and d at 5 [1]. 35 iterations were simulated in each trial; 20 trials were run. During each round, each agent (network node) plays one game (16 concepts) with one of its neighbors. The order of neighbors is shuffled initially, but constant across the rounds. A variable *Round* coded iterations from $1to35$.

Results Figure 3 shows the learning curve for agent pairs in the four networks. Agents in all networks converge. Confidence intervals obtained via bootstrapping indicated no apparent differences at any specific iteration. A linear model was fitted estimating the effects of network type overall (as a baseline) for each of the four types. It also fitted interactions of iteration (1–35) with the network types, which indicate significant learning effects as follows. For each network type, we found a significant learning effect (effect of *Round*) ($\beta\ 0.002, p < 0.001$).

Planned comparisons of the learning rate in Small World networks revealed no difference with either of the other three network types ($p > 0.3$).

[1] We found that networks need to be sufficiently large to display meaningful differences in community structure. The sizes were chosen to be computationally feasible (4h/CPU core per network).

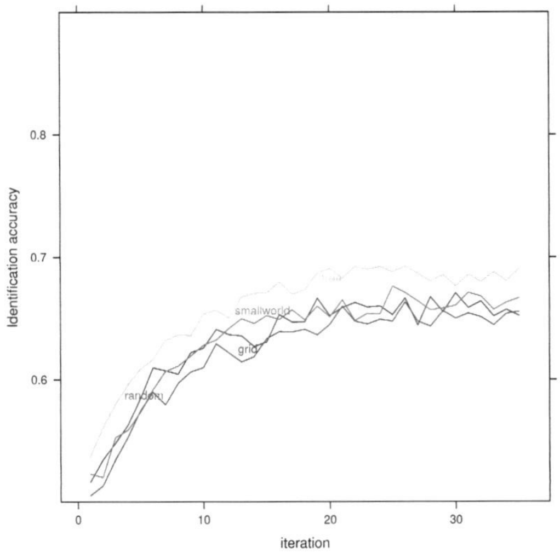

Figure 3: Identification accuracy between connected agents for communities of different network structures.

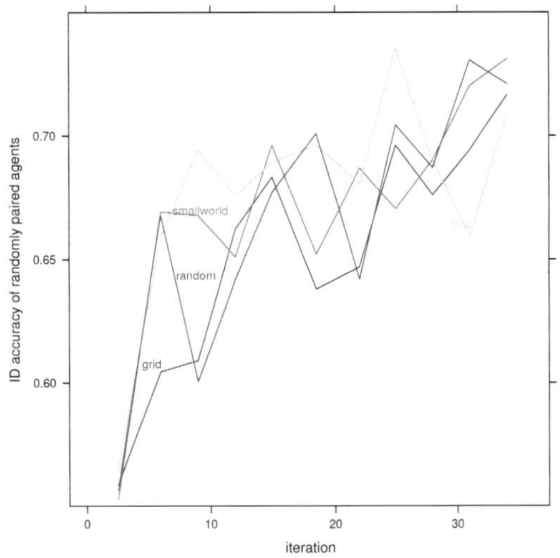

Figure 4: (Aggregate) Identification accuracy between random agent pairs for communities of different network structures.

5 Simulation 2

The success of a community is not only determined by how successfully individuals communicate in their local environment, that is, with their network neighbors. Communities require communicative success outside of well-acquainted agents. Agents' languages would ideally converge on a global scale. One way to test this is to have randomly paired agents play the Pictionary game at regular intervals throughout the game and thus measure identification accuracy outside of the network that defines the social structure.

This simulation was identical to Simulation 1, except that we scaled up the simulation to examine whether the lack of effect was possibly due to size or density of the nodes ($N = 512, d = 6$, noise level: 0.2, repetitions: 20). In this simulation, we measured ID accuracy between pairs of randomly chosen agents after each round. For three network types, *Grid*, *Small World* and *Random* we found significant interactions with *round*, i.e. significant convergence, (all $\beta > 0.016, z > 2.1, p < 0.05$). For the network type *Tree* we found no significant interaction ($\beta = 0.012, z = 1.55, p = 0.12$).[2]

To test the initial hypothesis, we re-coded the conditions with a *SmallWorld* factor, contrasting the small world networks with all other conditions. We found an effect of *Round* ($\beta = 0.017, z = 3.66, p < 0.001$), indicating convergence, but no interaction with *SmallWorld* ($\beta = -0.00027, z = -0.03, p = 0.98$).[3]

Results Figure 4 shows network-global convergence. Again, a linear model was fitted to estimate the learning rate in different network types (interaction of network type and iteration) (baseline intercepts were fitted for each network type). We found significant interactions with iteration for the following network types: *Grid* ($\beta = 0.004, p < 0.001$), *Small World* ($\beta = 0.003, p < 0.01$), and *Random* ($\beta = 0.003, p < 0.005$), but not for *Tree* ($p = 0.991$).

Planned comparisons revealed an interaction of network type and iteration for *Tree* compared to *Small World* ($\beta = -0.003, p < 0.05$), but not for *Grid* nor *Random* compared to *Small World* ($p > 0.35$). This indicates slower across-network convergence for trees than for small worlds. It also suggests that convergence across the network does not differ much between grids, random networks and small worlds.

[2]All regressions in this simulation where (generalized) mixed-effects models, with ID accuracy as response via logit link, *Round* as predictor, and *Condition* as factor for four network types. A random intercept was fitted, grouped by repetition ($1 - 20$), to account for repeated measures. The predictor was centered; no substantial collinearity remained. The analysis of Simulation 1 was a simple linear model; ID accuracy was, for all levels, not near either extreme ($\mu = 0.77$).

[3]Further, unreported, experiments, showed a similar picture with a smaller network as in Simulation 1.

6 Discussion

We find that convergence is relatively stable across the four network types. Analyzing the differences between the networks, we find that the average degree, which was controlled for grids, random networks and small worlds, was substantially lower for trees ($d = 1.9$) due to the large number of leaves with degree 1. This (or the correlated algebraic connectivity of the network) may prove to be a deciding correlate with cross-network convergence. Other metrics, such as the clustering coefficient (Watts and Strogatz, 1998), which gives an indication of the degree of neighborhood cohesion

We see these results still as preliminary. More work needs to be done to investigate how well learning scales with network growth, and how network analytics such as clustering coefficients affect the dispersion of information.

Further work will explore range of networks and the possibly unique suitability of human learning mechanisms to succeed in such networks. We will explore the (subsymbolic) parameters governing adaptation, and to what extend the quantitative parameters we find universal to humans are substantially optimized to deal with the small-world networks and pareto degree-distributions found in human communities.

7 Conclusion

Cognition may appear to be adapted to the social structures prevalent in communities of flocks, packs and human teams. There are many reasons why such social structures themselves could have evolved; if cognitive constraints play a role, we expect it to be only a small factor among many. The present simulation results certainly do not support this view: they are much more compatible with a *humans-as-generalists* theory that proposes that humans have evolved to handle a variety of network structures well, or that their recency- and frequency-based learning mechanism is not specialized.

Learning, if adapted to social structure in any way, may go beyond the current, mechanistic and implicit mechanisms implemented in ACT-R and comparable theories: learning may rely on more explicit strategies, analyzing one's interaction partners and their current knowledge, and it needs to judge information according to its sources (*trust*). Meta-cognition could also play a role in determining when a set of signs is substantially novel and better than the current system, and thus worth enduring the cost of switching from a settled set of language conventions.

We have evaluated only a small, initial part of a co-evolution theory we proposed. Also, the problem we describe may be best operationalized at a higher abstraction level: *Consensus problems* and information spread have been intensively studied (e.g., Latora and Marchiori, 2001; Wu et al., 2004). Comparing community convergence in a number of differently-structured networks, so far we see little evidence supporting our hypothesis, namely that cognition (memory) has specialized to accommodate social structures as defined by contemporary network science, and that those structures accommodate cognitive properties. Instead, we find that the simulated cognitive agents converge in their communication systems quite well regardless of the network structures, at least as long as those networks are relatively small and of similar average degrees.

Acknowledgments

This work was funded by the Air Force Office of Scientific Research (MURI grant FA95500810356).

References

Anderson, J. R., Bothell, D., Byrne, M. D., Douglass, S., Lebiere, C., and Quin, Y. (2004). An integrated theory of mind. *Psychological Review*, 111:1036–1060.

Ball, J., Heiberg, A., and Silber, R. (2007). Toward a large-scale model of language comprehension in act-r 6. In *Proceedings of the 8th International Conference on Cognitive Modeling*, Ann Arbor, MI.

Barabasi, A. L. and Albert, R. (1999). Emergence of scaling in random networks. *Science*, 286(5439):509–512.

Brighton, H., Smith, K., and Kirby, S. (2005). Language as an evolutionary system. *Physics of Life Reviews*, 2(3):177–226.

Budiu, R. and Anderson, J. R. (2002). Comprehending anaphoric metaphors. *Memory & Cognition*, 30:158–165.

Christiansen, M. H. and Chater, N. (2008). Language as shaped by the brain. *Behavioral and Brain Sciences*, 31(5):489–509.

Crescentini, C. and Stocco, A. (2005). Agrammatism as a failure in the lexical activation process. In *Proceedings of the 27th Annual Conference of the Cognitive Science Society*.

Dall'Asta, L., Baronchelli, A., Barrat, A., and Loreto, V. (2006). Agreement dynamics on small-world networks. *EPL (Europhysics Letters)*, 73(6):969.

Erdős, P. and Rényi, A. (1959). On random graphs. I. *Publ. Math. Debrecen*, 6:290–297.

Fay, N., Garrod, S., and Roberts, L. (2008). The fitness and functionality of culturally evolved communication systems. *Philosophical Transactions of the Royal Society B: Biological Sciences*, 363(1509):3553–3561.

Fay, N., Garrod, S., Roberts, L., and Swoboda, N. (2010). The interactive evolution of human communication systems. *Cognitive Science*, 34(3):351–386.

Garrod, S. and Doherty, G. M. (1994). Conversation, co-ordination and convention: An empirical investigation of how groups establish linguistic conventions. *Cognition*, 53:181–215.

Garrod, S., Fay, N., Lee, J., Oberlander, J., and Macleod, T. (2007). Foundations of representation: Where might graphical symbol systems come from? *Cognitive Science*, 31(6):961–987.

Griffiths, T. L. and Kalish, M. L. (2007). Language evolution by iterated learning with Bayesian agents. *Cognitive Science*, 31(3):441–480.

Kirby, S. and Hurford, J. (2002). The emergence of linguistic structure: An overview of the iterated learning model. In Cangelosi, A. and Parisi, D., editors, *Simulating the Evolution of Language*, chapter 6, pages 121–148. Springer Verlag, London.

Laird, J. E. and Rosenbloom, P. S. (1987). Soar: An architecture for general intelligence. *Artificial Intelligence*, 33(1):1–64.

Latora, V. and Marchiori, M. (2001). Efficient behavior of small-world networks. *Phys. Rev. Lett.*, 87(19):198701.

Lewis, R. L. and Vasishth, S. (2005). An activation-based model of sentence processing as skilled memory retrieval. *Cognitive Science*, 29:1–45.

Pickering, M. J. and Garrod, S. (2004). Toward a mechanistic psychology of dialogue. *Behavioral and Brain Sciences*, 27:169–225.

Reitter, D. (2008). *Context Effects in Language Production: Models of Syntactic Priming in Dialogue Corpora*. PhD thesis, University of Edinburgh.

Reitter, D. and Lebiere, C. (2009). Towards explaining the evolution of domain languages with cognitive simulation. In *Proceedings of the 9th International Conference on Cognitive Modeling (ICCM)*, Manchester, UK.

Reitter, D. and Lebiere, C. (subm.). Towards explaining the evolution of domain languages with cognitive simulation. *Cognitive Systems Research*.

Reitter, D. and Moore, J. D. (2007). Predicting success in dialogue. In *Proceedings of the 45th Annual Meeting of the Association of Computational Linguistics (ACL)*, pages 808–815, Prague, Czech Republic.

Steedman, M. (2000). *The Syntactic Process*. MIT Press, Cambridge, MA.

Sun, R. (2001). Cognitive science meets multiagent systems: A prolegomenon. *Philosophical Psychology*, 14(1):5–28.

Watts, D. J. and Strogatz, S. H. (1998). Collective dynamics of /'small-world/' networks. *Nature*, 393(6684):440–442.

Wu, F., Huberman, B. A., Adamic, L. A., and Tyler, J. R. (2004). Information flow in social groups. *Physica A: Statistical and Theoretical Physics*, 337(1-2):327 – 335.

Is there syntactic adaptation in language comprehension?

Alex B. Fine, Ting Qian, T. Florian Jaeger and **Robert A. Jacobs**
Department of Brain and Cognitive Sciences
University of Rochester
Rochester, NY, USA
{afine, tqian, fjaeger, robbie}@bcs.rochester.edu

Abstract

In this paper we investigate the manner in which the human language comprehension system adapts to shifts in probability distributions over syntactic structures, given experimentally controlled experience with those structures. We replicate a classic reading experiment, and present a model of the behavioral data that implements a form of Bayesian belief update over the course of the experiment.

1 Introduction

One of the central insights to emerge from experimental psycholinguistics over the last half century is that human language comprehension and production are *probability-sensitive*. During language comprehension, language users exploit probabilistic information in the linguistic signal to make inferences about the speaker's most likely intended message. In syntactic comprehension specifically, comprehenders exploit statistical information about lexical and syntactic co-occurrence statistics. For instance, (1) is temporarily ambiguous at the noun phrase *the study*, since the NP can be parsed as either the direct object (DO) of the verb *acknowledge* or as the subject NP of a sentence complement (SC).

(1) The reviewers acknowledged the study...

- DO: ... in the journal.
- SC: ... had been revolutionary.

The ambiguity in the SC continuation is resolved at *had been*, which rules out the direct object interpretation of *the study*. Reading times at *had been*—the so-called point of disambiguation—are correlated with a variety of lexical-syntactic probabilities. For instance, if the probability of a SC is low, given the verb, subjects are *garden-pathed* and will display longer reading times at *had been*. Conversely, if the probability of a SC is high, the material at the point of disambiguation is relatively unsurprising (i.e. conveys less information), and reading times will be short. Readers are also sensitive to the probability of the post-verbal NP occurring as the direct object of the verb. This is often discussed in terms of *plausibility*—in (1), *the study* is a plausible direct object of *acknowledge* (relative to, say, *the window*), which will also contribute to longer reading times in the event of a SC continuation (Garnsey et al., 1997).

Thus, humans make pervasive use of probabilistic cues in the linguistic signal. A question that has received very little attention, however, is how language users maintain or update their representations of the probability distributions relevant to language use, given new evidence—a phenomenon we will call *adaptation*. That is, while we know that language users have access to linguistic statistics, we know little about the dynamics of this knowledge in language users: is the probabilistic information relevant to comprehension derived from experience during a critical period of language acquisition, or do comprehenders update their knowledge on the basis of experience throughout adulthood? *A priori*, both scenarios seem plausible—given the sheer number of cues relevant to comprehension, it would be advantageous to limit the resources devoted to acquiring this knowledge; on the other hand, any learner's linguistic experience is bound to be incomplete, so the ability to adapt to novel distributional patterns in the linguistic input may prove to be equally useful. The goal of this paper is to explore this issue and to take an initial step toward providing a computational framework for characterizing adaptation in language processing.

1.1 Adaptation in Sentence Comprehension

Both over time and across situations, humans are exposed to linguistic evidence that, in principle,

Proceedings of the 2010 Workshop on Cognitive Modeling and Computational Linguistics, ACL 2010, pages 18–26,
Uppsala, Sweden, 15 July 2010.

ought to lead to shifts in our representations of the relevant probability distributions. An efficient language processing system is expected to take new evidence into account so that behavior (decisions during online production, predictions about upcoming words, etc.) will be guided by accurate estimates of these probability distributions. At least at the level of phonetic perception and production, there is evidence that language users quickly adapt to the statistical characteristics of the ambient language. For instance, over the course of a single interaction, the speech of two interlocutors becomes more acoustically similar, a phenomenon known as spontaneous phonetic imitation (Goldinger, 1998). Perhaps even more strikingly, Clayards et al. (2008) demonstrated that, given a relatively small number of tokens, comprehenders shift the degree to which they rely on an acoustic cue as the *variance* of that cue changes, reflecting adaptation to the distributions of probabilistic cues in speech perception.

At the level of syntactic processing, belief update/adaptation has only recently been addressed (Wells et al., 2009; Snider and Jaeger, in prep). In this study, we examine adaptation at the level of syntactic comprehension. We provide a computational model of short- to medium-term adaptation to local shifts in the statistics of the input. While the Bayesian model presented can account for the behavioral data, the quality of the model depends on how control variables are treated. We discuss the theoretical and methodological implications of this result.

Section 2 describes the behavioral experiment, a slight modification of the classic reading experiment reported in Garnsey et al. (1997). The study reported in section 3 replicates the basic findings of (Garnsey et al., 1997). In sections 4 and 5 we outline a Bayesian model of syntactic adaptation, in which distributions over syntactic structures are updated at each trial based on the evidence in that trial, and discuss the relationship between the model results and control variables. Section 6 concludes.

2 Behavioral Experiment

2.1 Participants

Forty-six members of the university community participated in a self-paced reading study for payment. All were native speakers of English with normal or corrected to normal vision, based on self-report.

2.2 Materials

Subjects read a total of 98 sentences, of which 36 were critical items containing DO/SC ambiguities, as in (1). These 36 sentences comprise a subset of those used in Garnsey et al. (1997). The stimuli were manipulated along two dimensions: first, verbs were chosen such that the conditional probability of a SC, given the verb, varied. In Garnsey et al. (1997), this conditional probability was estimated from a norming study, in which subjects completed sentence fragments containing DO/SC verbs (e.g. *the lawyer acknowledged...*). We adopt standard psycholinguistic terminology and refer to this conditional probability as SC-bias. The verbs used in the critical sentences in Garnsey et al. (1997) were selected to span a wide range of SC-bias values, from .01 to .9. Each sentence contained a different DO/SC verb. In addition to SC-bias, half of the sentences presented to each subject included the complementizer *that*, as in (2).

(2) The reviewers acknowledged that the study had been revolutionary.

Sentences with a complementizer were included as an unambiguous baseline (Garnsey et al. 1997). The presence of a complementizer was counterbalanced, such that each subject saw half of the sentences with a complementizer and all sentences occurred with and without a complementizer equally often across subjects. All of the critical sentences contained a SC continuation. The 36 critical items were interleaved with 72 fillers that included simple transitives and intransitives.

2.3 Procedure

Subjects read critical and filler sentences in a self-paced moving window display (Just et al., 1982), presented using the Linger experimental presentation software (Rohde, 2005). Sentences were presented in a noncumulative word-by-word self-paced moving window. At the beginning of each trial, the sentence appeared on the screen with all non-space characters replaced by a dash. Using their dominant hands, subjects pressed the space bar to view each consecutive word in the sentence. Durations between space bar presses were recorded. At each press of the space bar, the currently-viewed word reverted to dashes as the next word was converted to letters. A yes/no comprehension question followed all experimental and filler sentences.

2.4 Analysis

In keeping with standard procedure, we used length-corrected residual per-word reading times as our dependent measure. Following Garnsey et al. (1997), we define the point of disambiguation in the critical sentences as the two words following the post-verbal NP (e.g. *had been* in (1) and (2)). All analyses reported here were conducted on residual reading times at this region. For a given subject, residual reading times more than two standard deviations from that subject's mean residual reading time were excluded.

3 Study 1

Residual reading times at the point of disambiguation were fit to a linear mixed effects regression model. This model included the full factorial design (i.e. all main effects and all interactions) of logged SC-bias (taken from the norming study reported in Garnsey et al. 1997) and complementizer presence. Additionally, the model included random intercepts of subject and item. This was the maximum random effect structure justified by the data, based on comparison against more complex models.[1] All predictors in the model were centered at zero in order to reduce collinearity. P-values reported in all subsequent models were calculated using MCMC sampling (where N = 10,000).

3.1 Results

This model replicated the findings reported by Garnsey et al. (1997). There was a significant main effect of complementizer presence ($\beta = -3.2, t = -2.5, p < .05$)—reading times at the point of disambiguation were lower when the complementizer was present. Additionally, there was a significant two-way interaction between complementizer presence and logged SC-bias ($\beta = 3.0, t = 2.5, p < .05$)—SC-bias has a stronger negative correlation with reading times in the disambiguating region when the complementizer is *absent*, as expected. Additionally, Garnsey et al. (1997) found a main effect of SC-bias. For us, this main effect did not reach significance ($\beta = -1.2, t = -1.11, p = .5$), possibly owing to the fact that we tested a much smaller sample than Garnsey et al. (1997) (51 compared to 82 participants).

4 Study 2: Bayesian Syntactic Adaptation

Reading times at the point of disambiguation in these stimuli reflect, among other things, subjects' estimates of the conditional probability $p(SC|verb)$ (Garnsey et al. 1997), which we have been calling SC-bias. Thus, we model the task facing subjects in this experiment as one of Bayesian inference, where subjects are, when reading a sentence containing the verb v_i, inferring a posterior probability $\mathrm{P}(SC|v_i)$, i.e. the probability that a sentence complement clause will follow a verb v_i. According to Bayes rule, we have:

$$p(SC|v_i) = \frac{p(v_i|SC)p(SC)}{p(v_i)} \qquad (1)$$

In Equation (1), we use the relative frequency of v_i (estimated from the British National Corpus) as the estimate for $p(v_i)$. The first term in the numerator, $p(v_i|SC)$, is the likelihood, which we estimate by using the relative frequency of v_i among all verbs that can take a sentence complement as their argument. These values are taken from the corpus study by Roland et al. (2007). Roland et al. (2007) report, among other things, the number of times a SC occurs as the argument of roughly 200 English verbs. These values are reported across a number of corpora. We use the values from the BNC to compute $p(v_i|SC)$.

The prior probability of a sentence complement clause, $p(SC)$, is the estimate of interest in this study. We hypothesize that, under the assumptions of the current model, subjects update their estimate for $p(SC)$ based on the evidence presented in each trial. As a result, the posterior probability varies from trial to trial, not only because the verb used in each stimulus is different, but also because the belief about the probability of a sentence complement is being updated based on the evidence in each trial. We employ the beta-binomial model to simulate this updating process, as described next.

4.1 Belief Update

We adopt an online training paradigm involving an ideal observer learning from observations. After observing a sentence containing a DO/SC verb,

[1] For a detailed description of the procedure used, see http://hlplab.wordpress.com/2009/05/14/random-effect-should-i-stay-or-should-i-go/

we predict that subjects will update both the likelihood $p(v_i|SC)$ for that verb, as well as the probability $p(SC)$. Because each verb occurs only once for a given subject, the effect of updating the first quantity is impossible to measure in the current experimental paradigm. We therefore focus on modeling how subjects update their belief of $p(SC)$ from trial to trial.

We make the simplifying assumption that the only possible argument that DO/SC verbs can take is either a direct object or a sentence complement clause. Further, subjects are assumed to have an initial belief about how probable a sentence complement is, on a scale of 0 to 1. Let θ denote this probability estimate, and $p(\theta)$ the strength of this estimate. From the perspective of an ideal observer, $p(\theta)$ will go up for $\theta > 0.5$ when a DO/SC verb is presented with a sentence complement as its argument. This framework assumes that subjects do not compute θ by merely relying on frequency (otherwise, θ will be simply the ratio between SC and DO structures in a block of trials), but they have a distribution $P(\theta)$, where each possible estimate of θ is associated with a probability indicating the confidence on that estimate. In order to make our results comparable to existing models, however, we use the expected value of $P(\theta)$ in each iteration of training as point estimates. Therefore, for one subject, we have 36 estimated $\hat{\theta}$ values, each corresponding to the changed belief after seeing a sentence containing SC in an experiment of 36 trials. Because none of the filler items included DO/SC verbs, we assume that filler trials have no effect on subjects' estimates of $P(\theta)$.

Since all stimuli in our experiment have the SC structure, the general expectation is the distribution $P(\theta)$ will shift towards the end where $\theta = 1$. Our belief update model tries to capture the shape of this shift during the course of the experiment. Using Bayesian inference, we can describe the updating process as the following, where θ_i represents a particular belief of the value θ.

$$\begin{aligned} p(\theta = \theta_i|obs.) &= \frac{p(obs.|\theta = \theta_i)p(\theta = \theta_i)}{p(obs.)} \\ &= \frac{p(obs.|\theta = \theta_i)p(\theta = \theta_i)}{\int_0^1 p(obs.|\theta)p(\theta)\, d\theta} \end{aligned} \tag{2}$$

This posterior probability is hypothesized to reflect how likely a subject would consider the probability of SC to be θ_i after being exposed to one experimental item. We discretized θ to 100 evenly spaced θ_i values, ranging from 0 to 1. Thus, the denominator can be calculated by marginalizing over the 100 θ_i values. The two terms in the numerator in Equation (2) are estimated in the following manner.

Likelihood function $p(obs.|\theta = \theta_i)$ is modeled by a binomial distribution, where the parameters are θ_i (the probability of observing a SC clause) and $1 - \theta_i$ (the probability of observing a direct object), and where the outcome is the experimental item presented to the subject. Therefore:

$$p(obs.|\theta = \theta_i) = \frac{(n_{sc} + n_{do})!}{n_{sc}! n_{do}!} \theta_i^{n_{sc}} (1 - \theta_i)^{n_{do}} \tag{3}$$

In the current experiment, n_{do} is always 0 since all stimuli contain the SC argument. In addition, between-trial reading time differences are modelled at one item a step for each subject so that n_{sc} is always 1 in each trial. It is in theory possible to set n_{sc} to other numbers.

The prior In online training, the posterior of the previous iteration is used as the prior for the current one. Nevertheless, the prior $p(\theta = \theta_i)$ for the very first iteration of training needs to be estimated. Here we assume a beta distribution with parameters α and β. The probability of the prior then is:

$$p(\theta = \theta_i) = \frac{\theta_i^{\alpha-1}(1 - \theta_i)^{\beta-1}}{B(\alpha, \beta)}$$

Intuitively, α and β capture the number of times subjects have observed the SC and DO outcomes, respectively, before the experiment. In the context of our research, this model assumes that subjects' beliefs about $p(SC)$ and $p(DO)$ are based on $\alpha - 1$ observations of SC and $\beta - 1$ observations of DO prior to the experiment.

The values of the parameters of the beta distribution were obtained by searching through the parameter space with an objective function based on the Bayesian information criterion (BIC) score of a regression model containing the log of the posterior computed using the updated prior $p(SC)$, complementizer presence, and the two-way interaction. The BIC (Schwarz, 1978) is a measure of model quality that weighs the models empirical coverage against its parsimony ($BIC = 2ln(\mathcal{L}) +$

$k * ln(n)$, where k is the number of parameters in the model, n the number of data points, and $\mathcal{L}$ is the models data likelihood). Smaller BIC indicate better models. The α and β values yielding the lowest BIC score are used.

In estimating α and β, we considered all pairs of non-negative integers such that both values were below 1000. The values of α and β used here were 1 and 177, respectively. These values do not imply that subjects have seen only 1 SC and 177 DOs prior to the experiment, but that only this many observations inform subjects' prior beliefs about this distribution. The relationship between the choice of the parameters of the beta distribution, α and β, and the BIC of the model used in the parameter estimation is shown in Figure 1.

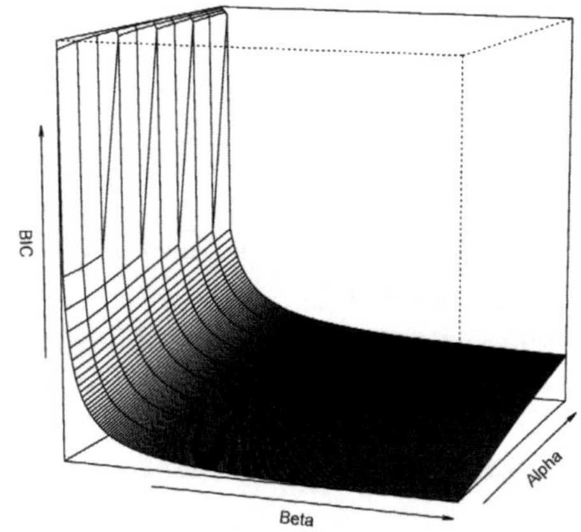

Figure 1: The relationship between the BIC of the model used in the parameter estimation step and values of α and β in the beta distribution

Because we model subjects' estimates of $p(SC|v_i)$ in terms of Bayesian inference, with a continuously updated prior, $p(SC)$, the value of $p(SC|v_i)$ depends, in our model, on both verb-specific statistics (i.e. the likelihood $p(v_i|SC)$ and the probability of the verb $p(v_i)$) and the point in the experiment at which the trial containing that verb is encountered. We can visualize this relationship in Figure 2, which shows the values given by the model of $p(SC|v_i)$ for four particular different verbs, depending on the point in the experiment at which the verb is seen.

The approach we take is hence fundamentally

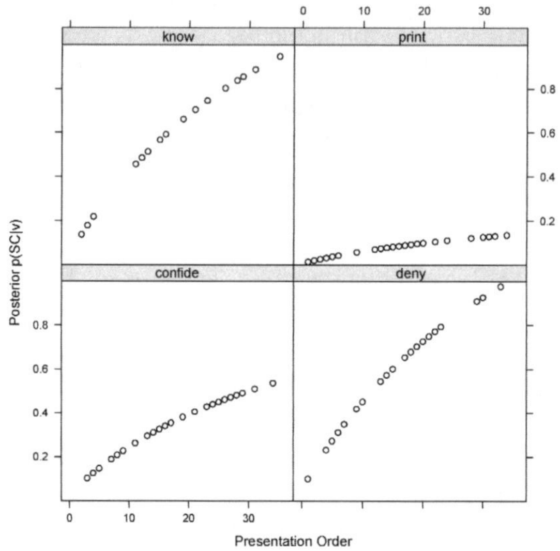

Figure 2: The relationship, for four of the verbs, between the value of $p(SC|v_i)$ given by the model as a function of *when* in the experiment v_i is encountered

different from the approach commonly taken in psycholinguistics, which is to use static estimates of quantities such as $p(SC|v_i)$ derived from corpora or norming studies.

4.2 Analysis

To test whether the model-derived values of $p(SC|v_i)$ are a good fit for the behavioral data, we fit residual reading times at the point of disambiguation using linear mixed effects regression. The model included main effects of $p(SC|v_i)$—as given by the model just described—and complementizer presence, as well as the two-way interaction between these two predictors. Additionally, there were random intercepts of subject and item. $p(SC|v_i)$ was logged and centered at zero.

4.3 Results

There was a highly significant main effect of the posterior probability $p(SC|v_i)$ yielded by the beta-binomial model ($\beta = -40, t = -21.2, p < .001$), as well as a main effect of complementizer presence ($-4.5, t = -3.7, p < .001$). The two-way interaction between complementizer presence and the posterior probability from the beta-binomial model did not reach significance ($\beta = 0.5, t = .5, p > .05$). The reason is likely that, in the analysis presented for Study 1, we can interpret the interaction as indicating that when

SC-bias is high, the complementizer has less of an effect; in our model, the posterior probability $p(SC|v_i)$ is both generally higher and has less variance than the same quantity when based on corpus- or norming study estimates, since the prior probability $p(SC)$ is continuously increasing over the course of the experiment. This would have the effect of eliminating or at least obscuring the interaction with complementizer presence.

The posterior $p(SC|v_i)$ has a much stronger negative correlation with residual reading times than the measure of SC-bias used in Study 1 ($\beta = -40$ as opposed to $\beta = -1.2$).

4.4 Discussion

So far, we have replicated a classic finding in the sentence processing literature (Study 1), provided evidence that subjects' estimates of the conditional probability $p(SC|v_i)$ change based on evidence throughout the experiment, and that this process is captured well by a model which implements a form of incremental Bayesian belief update. We take this as evidence that the language comprehension system is *adaptive*, in the sense that language users continually update their estimates of probability distributions over syntactic structures.

5 Syntactic Adaptation vs. Motor Adaptation

The results of the model presented in section 4 are amenable to (at least) two explanations. We have hypothesized that, given exposure to new evidence about probability distributions over syntactic structures in English, subjects update their beliefs about these probability distributions, reflected in reading times—a phenomenon we refer to as syntactic adaptation. An alternative explanation, however, is one that appeals to *motor* adaptation, rather than syntactic adaptation. Specifically, it could be that subjects are simply adapting to the task—rather than to changes in syntactic distributions—as the experiment proceeds, leading to faster reading times.

We expect the effect of motor adaptation to be captured by *presentation order*, or the point in the experiment at which subjects encounter a given stimulus. In particular, we predict a negative correlation between presentation order and reading times. Unfortunately, in the current experiment, presentation order and $p(SC|v_i)$ derived from the Beta-binomial model are positively correlated ($r = .6$)—the latter increases with increasing presentation order, since participants only see SC continuations. The results we observed above could hence also be due to an effect of presentation order.

The expected *shape* of a possible effect of task adaptation is not obvious. That is, it is not clear whether the relationship between presentation order and reading times will be linear. On the one hand, linearity would be the default assumption prior to theoretical considerations about the distributional properties of presentation order. On the other hand, presentation order is a lower-bounded variable, which often are distributed approximately log-normally. Additionally, it is possible that there may be a floor effect: participants may get used to having to press the space bar to advance to the next word and may quickly get faster at that procedure until RTs converge against the minimal time it takes to program the motor movement to press the space bar. Such an effect would likely lead to an approximately log-linear effect of presentation order.

We test for an effect of motor adaptation by examining the effect of presentation order on reading times, comparing the effect of linear and log-transformed presentation order.

5.1 Controlling for Presentation Order in the Beta-binomial model

We test for separate effects of syntactic adaptation and motor adaptation by conducting stepwise regressions with two models containing the full factorial design of the Beta-binomial posterior, complementizer presence, and, for the first model, a linear effect of presentation order and, for the second model, log-transformed presentation order. We conducted stepwise regressions using backward elimination, starting with all predictors and removing non-significant predictors (i.e. $p > .1$), one at a time, until all non-significant predictors are deleted.

For both the model including a linear effect of presentation order and a model including log-transformed presentation order, the final models resulting from the stepwise regression procedure included only main effects of complementizer presence and log presentation order. These models are summarized in Figure 1, which includes coefficient-based tests for significance of each of the predictors (i.e. whether the coefficient is significantly different from zero) as well as χ^2-based tests for significance (i.e. the difference between a model with that predictor and one without). Comparing the two resulting models based on the Bayesian Information Criterion, the model containing log-transformed presentation order is a better model than one with a linear effect of presentation order ($BIC_{log} = 37467$; $BIC_{non-log} = 37510$).

Pres. order untransformed				
Coef. and χ^2-based tests				
Predictor	β	p	χ^2	p
Comp. pres.	-4.3	$< .05$	4.9	$< .05$
Pres. order	$-.7$	$< .001$	28.2	$< .001$
Pres. order log-transformed				
Coef. and χ^2-based tests				
Predictor	β	p	χ^2	p
Comp. pres.	-4.3	$< .05$	4.8	$< .05$
Pres. order	-33.8	$< .001$	29.4	$< .001$

Table 1: Coefficient- and χ^2-based tests for significance of model resulting from stepwise regression

In sum, the beta-binomial derived posterior appears to have no predictive power after presentation order is controlled for. This result does not depend on how presentation order is treated (i.e. log-transformed or not).

5.2 The interaction between SC-bias and presentation order

The results from the previous section suggest that the Beta-binomial derived posterior carries no predictive power after presentation order is controlled for. Is there any evidence at all for syntactic adaptation (as opposed to motor, or task, adaptation)?

To attempt to answer this, we analyzed the reading data using the model reported in section 3, with an additional main effect of presentation order, as well as the interactions between presentation order and the other predictors in the model. An overall decrease in reading times due to motor adaptation should surface as a main effect of presentation order, as mentioned; syntactic adaptation, however, is predicted to show up as a two-way interaction between SC-bias and presentation order—since subjects only see SC continuations, subjects should expect this outcome to become more and more probable over the course of the experiment, causing the correlation between SC-bias and reading times to become weaker (thus we predict the interaction to have a positive coefficient).

To test for such an interaction, we performed a stepwise regressions with two models containing the full factorial design of SC-bias, complementizer presence, and, for the first model, a linear effect of presentation order and, for the second model, log-transformed presentation order. The stepwise regression procedure here was identical to the one reported in the previous section.

For both models, the remaining predictors were main effects of presentation order, complementizer presence, and SC-bias, as well as a two-way interaction between SC-bias and complementizer presence and a two-way interaction between SC-bias and presentation order. The results of these models are given in Table 2.

Pres. order untransformed				
Coef. and χ^2-based tests				
Predictor	β	p	χ^2	p
SC-bias	$-.4$	$= .8$	11.5	$< .001$
Comp. pres.	-4.4	$< .001$	18.1	$< .001$
Pres. order	$-.9$	$< .001$	420.9	$< .001$
SC-bias:Comp.	2.6	$< .05$	5.3	$< .05$
SC-bias:Pres. Order	$.1$	$< .05$	6.2	$< .05$
Pres. order log-transformed				
Coef. and χ^2-based tests				
Predictor	β	p	χ^2	p
SC-bias	-1.4	$= .5$	8.9	$< .05$
Comp. pres.	-4.6	$< .001$	19.3	$< .001$
Pres. order	-42.4	$< .001$	461.2	$< .001$
SC-bias:Comp.	2.6	$< .05$	5.2	$< .05$
SC-bias:Pres. Order	3.5	$= .06$	3.4	$= .06$

Table 2: Coefficient- and χ^2-based tests for significance of model resulting from stepwise regression

The main findings reported in Study 1 (i.e. a main effect of complementizer presence and a two-way interaction between SC-bias and complementizer presence) are replicated here, and do not depend on whether presentation order is log-transformed. However, the interaction between SC-bias and presentation order is less reliable when presentation order is log-transformed, reaching only marginal significance. In short, an adequate account of the data requires reference to both motor adaptation (in the form of a main effect of presentation order, log-transformed) and syntactic adaptation.

If subjects are improving at the task, and the effect of presentation order represents a kind of adaptation to the task of self-paced reading, we would expect to find a main effect of presentation order on reading times at *all* regions. This is the case—a strong negative correlation between presentation order and reading times holds across all regions. Evidence that the observed interaction is due to syntactic belief update comes from the fact that the interaction between SC-bias and presentation order, unlike the main effect of presentation order, is *limited to the disambiguating region of the sentence*. We performed the regression reported above on residual reading times at the main verb (e.g. *acknowledge*), ambiguous (e.g. *the study*), and disambiguating (e.g. *had been*) regions. These analyses revealed, as expected, main effects of presentation order across all regions. At the verb and ambiguous regions, however, presentation order did not interact with SC-bias.

Region	β	$p-value$
Main effect of pres. order		
Verb	$-.95$	$< .001$
Ambig. region	$-.9$	$< .001$
Disambig. region	$-.9$	$< .001$
Pres. order X SC-bias interaction		
Verb	.09	$= .24$
Ambig. region	.04	$= .37$
Disambig. region	.1	$< .05$

Table 3: Main effect of presentation order and interaction of presentation order with SC-bias at different regions in the critical sentences

This finding provides initial evidence that subjects adapt their linguistic expectations to the evidence observed throughout the experiment. However, the interaction between presentation order and SC-bias in this analysis is amenable to an alternative interpretation: interactions between presentation order and other variables could emerge if subjects' reaction times reach some minimum value over the course of the experiment, causing any other variable to become less strongly correlated with the dependent measure as reaction times approach that minimum value. Thus this interaction could be an artefact of a *floor effect*.

To test the possibility that the SC-bias-presentation order interaction is the result of a floor effect, we compared the 1st, 5th, and 10th fastest percentiles of residual reading times across all regions. As shown in Figure 3, faster reading times are observed at each quantile in at least one other region. In other words, reading times in the disambiguating region do not seem to be bounded by motor demands associated with the task. We hence tentatively conclude that the interaction between SC-bias and log-transformed presentation order is not the result of a floor effect, although this issue deserves further attention.

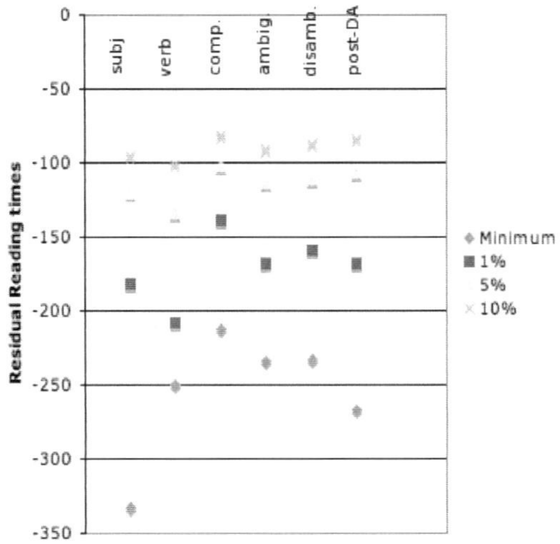

Figure 3: Minimum and upper boundary of 1st, 5th, and 10th percentile values of residual reading times across all sentence regions

6 Conclusion

We hypothesized that the language comprehension system rapidly adapts to shifts in the probability distributions over syntactic structures on the basis of experience with those structures. To investigate this phenomenon, we modelled reading times from a self-paced reading experiment using a Bayesian model of incremental belief update. While an initial test of the Beta-binomial model was encouraging, the predictions of the Beta-binomial model are highly correlated with presentation order in the current data set. This means that it is hard to distinguish between adaptation to the task of self-paced reading and syntactic adaptation. Indeed, model comparison suggests that the Bayesian model does not explain a significant amount of the variance in reading times once motor adaptation (as captured by stimulus presentation order) is accounted for. In a secondary analysis, we did, however, find preliminary evidence of syntactic adaptation. That is, while the Beta-binomial model does not seem to capture syntactic belief update adequately, there is evidence that comprehenders continuously update their syntactic distributions.

Teasing apart the effects of motor adaptation and linguistic adaptation will require experimental designs in which these two factors are not as highly correlated as in the present study. Ongoing work addresses this issue.

Acknowledgements

The authors wish to thank Neal Snider and members of the Human Language Processing lab, as well as three anonymous ACL reviewers for helpful discussion and feedback. We are also very grateful to Jeremy Ferris for help in collecting the data reported here. This work was supported by the University of Rochesters Provost Award for Multidisciplinary Research and NSF grant BCS-0845059 to TFJ.

References

John Anderson. 1990. *The adaptive character of thought*. Lawrence Erlbaum.

Bock and Griffin. 2000. The persistence of structural priming: Transient activation or implicit learning? *Journal of Experimental Psychology*, 129(2):177–192.

Chang, Dell, and Bock. 2006. Becoming syntactic. *Psychological Review*, 113(2):234–272.

Clayards, Tanenhaus, Aslin, and Jacobs. 2008. Perception of speech reflects optimal use of probabilistic cues. *Cognition*, 108:804–809.

Garnsey, Pearlmutter, Myers, and Lotocky. 1997. The contributions of verb bias and plausibility to the comprehension of temporarily ambiguous sentences. *Journal of Memory and Language*, (37):58–93.

S.D. Goldinger. 1998. Echoes of echoes? an episodic theory of lexical access. *Psychological Review*, (105):251–279.

Florian Jaeger. in press. Redundancy and reduction: speakers manage syntactic information density. *Cognitive Psychology*.

Just, Carpenter, and Woolley. 1982. Paradigms and processes in reading comprehension. *Journal of Experimental Psychology: General*, 111:228–238.

Rohde. 2005. Linger experiment presentation software. http://tedlab.mit.edu/ dr/Linger/.

Schwarz. 1978. Estimating the dimension of a model. *Annals of Statistics*, 6:461–464.

Herbert Simon, 1987. *77K New Palgrave Dictionary of Economics*, chapter Bounded Rationality, pages 266–268. Macmillan, London.

Neal Snider and Florian Jaeger. in prep.

Thothathiri and Snedeker. 2008. Give and take: Syntactic priming during language comprehension. *Cognition*, 108:51–68.

Wells, Christiansen, Race, Acheson, and MacDonald. 2009. Experience and sentence comprehension: Statistical learning and relative clause comprehension. *Cognitive Psychology*, 58:250–271.

HHMM Parsing with Limited Parallelism

Tim Miller
Department of Computer Science
and Engineering
University of Minnesota, Twin Cities
tmill@cs.umn.edu

William Schuler
University of Minnesota, Twin Cities
and The Ohio State University
schuler@ling.ohio-state.edu

Abstract

Hierarchical Hidden Markov Model (HHMM) parsers have been proposed as psycholinguistic models due to their broad coverage within human-like working memory limits (Schuler et al., 2008) and ability to model human reading time behavior according to various complexity metrics (Wu et al., 2010). But HHMMs have been evaluated previously only with very wide beams of several thousand parallel hypotheses, weakening claims to the model's efficiency and psychological relevance. This paper examines the effects of varying beam width on parsing accuracy and speed in this model, showing that parsing accuracy degrades gracefully as beam width decreases dramatically (to 2% of the width used to achieve previous top results), without sacrificing gains over a baseline CKY parser.

1 Introduction

Probabilistic parsers have been successful at accurately estimating syntactic structure from free text. Typically, these systems work by considering entire sentences (or utterances) at once, using dynamic programming to obtain globally optimal solutions from locally optimal sub-parses.

However, these methods usually do not attempt to conform to human-like processing constraints, e.g. leading to center embedding and garden path effects (Chomsky and Miller, 1963; Bever, 1970). For systems prioritizing accurate parsing performance, there is little need to produce human-like errors. But from a human modeling perspective, the success of globally optimized whole-utterance models raises the question of how humans can accurately parse linguistic input without access to this same global optimization. This question creates a niche in computational research for models that are able to parse accurately while adhering as closely as possible to human-like psycholinguistic constraints.

Recent work on incremental parsers includes work on Hierarchical Hidden Markov Model (HHMM) parsers that operate in linear time by maintaining a bounded store of incomplete constituents (Schuler et al., 2008). Despite this seeming limitation, corpus studies have shown that through the use of grammar transforms, this parser is able to cover nearly all sentences contained in the Penn Treebank (Marcus et al., 1993) using a small number of unconnected memory elements.

But this bounded-memory parsing comes at a price. The HHMM parser obtains good coverage within human-like memory bounds only by pursuing an 'optionally arc-eager' parsing strategy, nondeterministically guessing which constituents can be kept open for attachment (occupying an active memory element), or closed for attachment (freeing a memory element for subsequent constituents). Although empirically determining the number of parallel competing hypotheses used in human sentence processing is difficult, previous results in computational models have shown that human-like behavior can be elicited at very low levels of parallelism (Boston et al., 2008b; Brants and Crocker, 2000), suggesting that large numbers of active hypotheses are not needed. Previously, the HHMM parser has only been evaluated on large beam widths, leaving this aspect of its psycholinguistic plausibility untested.

In this paper, the performance of an HHMM parser will be evaluated in two experiments that

Proceedings of the 2010 Workshop on Cognitive Modeling and Computational Linguistics, ACL 2010, pages 27–35,
Uppsala, Sweden, 15 July 2010.

vary the amount of parallelism allowed during parsing, measuring the degree to which this degrades the system's accuracy. In addition, the evaluation will compare the HHMM parser to an off-the-shelf probabilistic CKY parser to evaluate the actual run time performance at various beam widths. This serves two purposes, evaluating one aspect of the plausibility of this parsing framework as a psycholinguistic model, and evaluating its potential utility as a tool for operating on unsegmented text or speech.

2 Related Work

There are several criteria a parser must meet in order to be plausible as a psycholinguistic model of the human sentence-processing mechanism (HSPM).

Incremental operation is perhaps the most obvious. The HSPM is able to process sentences incrementally, meaning that at each point in time of processing input, it has some hypothesis of the interpretation of that input, and each subsequent unit of input serves to update that hypothesis.

The next criterion for psycholinguistic plausibility is processing efficiency. The HSPM not only operates incrementally, but in standard operation it does not lag behind a speaker, even if, for example, the speaker continues speaking at extended length without pause. Standard machine approaches, such as chart parsers based on the CKY algorithm, operate in worst-case cubic run time on the length of input. Without knowing where an utterance or sentence might end, such an algorithm will take more time with each successive word and will eventually fall behind.

The third criterion is a reasonable limiting of memory resources. This constraint means that the HSPM, while possibly considering multiple hypotheses in parallel, is not limitlessly so, as evidenced by the existence of garden path sentences (Bever, 1970; Lewis, 2000). If this were not the case, garden-path sentences would not cause problems, as reaching the disambiguating word would simply result in a change in the favored hypothesis. In fact, garden path sentences typically cannot be understood on a first pass and must be reread, indicating that the correct analysis is attainable and yet not present in the set of parallel hypotheses of the first pass.

While parsers meeting these three criteria can claim to not violate any psycholinguistic constraints, there has been much recent work in testing psycholinguistically-motivated parsers to make forward predictions about human sentence processing, in order to provide positive evidence for certain probabilistic parsing models as valid psycholinguistic models of sentence processing. This work has largely focused on correlating measures of parsing difficulty in computational models with delays in reading time in human subjects.

Hale (2001) introduced the *surprisal* metric for probabilistic parsers, which measures the log ratio of the total probability mass at word $t-1$ and word t. In other words, it measures how much probability was lost in incorporating the next word into the current hypotheses. Boston et al. (2008a) show that surprisal is a significant predictor of reading time (as measured in self-paced reading experiments) using a probabilistic dependency parser. Roark et al. (2009) dissected parsing difficulty metrics (including surprisal and entropy) to separate out the effects of syntactic and lexical difficulties, and showed that these new metrics are strong predictors of reading difficulty.

Wu et al. (2010) evaluate the same Hierarchical Hidden Markov Model parser used in this work in terms of its ability to reproduce human-like results for various complexity metrics, including some of those mentioned above, and introduce a new metric called *embedding difference*. This metric is based on the idea of embedding depth, which is the number of elements in the memory store required to hold a given hypothesis. Using more memory elements corresponds to center embedding in phrase structure trees, and presumably correlates to some degree with complexity. Average embedding for a time step is computed by computing the weighted average number of required memory elements (weighted by probability) for all hypotheses on the beam. Embedding difference is simply the change in this value when the next word is encountered.

Outside of Wu et al., the most similar work from a modeling perspective is an incremental parser implemented using Cascaded Hidden Markov Models (CHMMs) (Crocker and Brants, 2000). This model is superficially similar to the Hierarchical Hidden Markov Models described below in that it relies on multiple levels of interdependent HMMs to account for hierarchical structure in an incremental model. Crocker and Brants use the system to parse ambiguous sentences (such as *the athlete realized his goals were out of reach*) and examine the relative probabilities of two plausible analyses at each time step. They then show that the shifting of these two probabilities is consistent with empirical evidence about how humans perceive these sentences word by word.

However, as will be described below, the HHMM has advantages over the CHMM from a psycholinguistic modeling perspective. The HHMM uses a limited memory store containing only four elements which is consistent with many estimates of human short term memory limits (Cowan, 2001; Miller, 1956). In addition to modeling memory limits, the limited store acts as a fixed-depth stack that ensures linear asymptotic parsing time, and a grammar transform allows for wide coverage of speech and newspaper corpora within that limited memory store (Schuler et al., 2010).

3 Hierarchical Hidden Markov Model Parser

Hidden Markov Models (HMMs) have long been used to successfully model sequence data in which there is a latent (hidden) variable at each time step that generates the observed evidence at that time step. These models are used for such applications as part-of-speech tagging, and speech recognition.

Hierarchical Hidden Markov Models (HHMMs) are an extension of HMMs which can represent sequential data containing hierarchical relations. In HHMMs, complex hidden variables may output evidence for several time steps in sequence. This process may recurse, though a finite depth is required to make any guarantees about performance. Murphy and Paskin (2001) showed that this model could be framed as a Dynamic Bayes Network (DBN), so that inference is linear on the length of the input sequence.

In the HHMM parser used here, the complex hidden variables are syntactic states that generate sub-sequences of other syntactic states, eventually generating pre-terminals and words. This section will describe how the trees must be transformed, and then mapped to HHMM states. This section will then continue with a formal definition of an HHMM, followed by a description of how this model can parse natural language, and finally a discussion of what different aspects of the model represent in terms of psycholinguistic modeling.

3.1 Right-Corner Transform

In order to parse with an HHMM, phrase structure trees need to be mapped to a hierarchical sequence of states of nested HMMs. Since Murphy and Paskin showed that the run time complexity of the HHMM is exponential on the depth of the nested HMMs, it is important to minimize the depth of the model for optimal performance. In order to do this, a tree transformation known as a *right-corner transform* is applied to the phrase structure trees comprising the training data, to transform right-expanding sequences of complete constituents into left-expanding sequences of incomplete constituents A_η/A_μ, consisting of an instance of an active constituent A_η lacking an instance of an awaited constituent A_μ yet to be recognized. This transform can be defined as a synchronous grammar that maps every context-free rule expansion in a source tree (in Chomsky Normal Form) to a corresponding expansion in a right-corner transformed tree:[1]

- Beginning case: the top of a right-expanding sequence in an ordinary phrase structure tree is mapped to the bottom of a left-expanding sequence in a right-corner transformed tree:

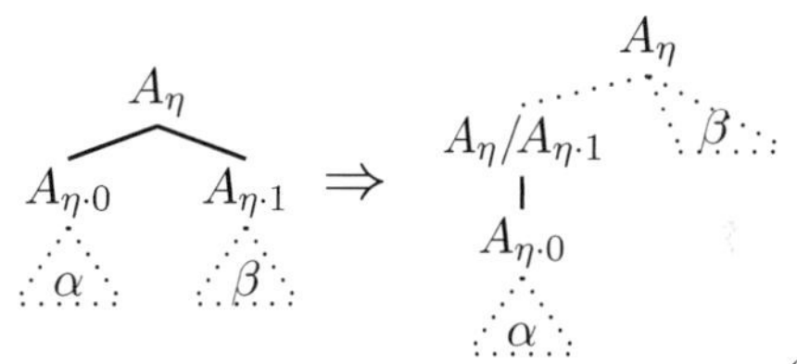

(1)

- Middle case: each subsequent branch in a right-expanding sequence of an ordinary phrase structure tree is mapped to a branch in a left-expanding sequence of the transformed tree:

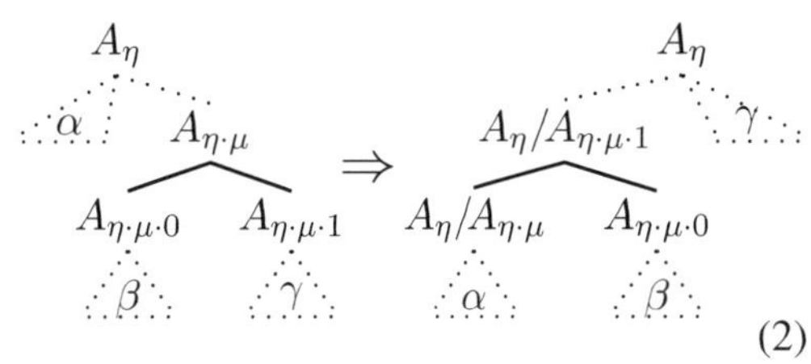

(2)

- Ending case: the bottom of a right-expanding sequence in an ordinary phrase structure tree

[1] Here, η and μ are tree node addresses, consisting of sequences of zeros, representing left branches, and ones, representing right branches, on a path from the root of the tree to any given node.

a)

b)

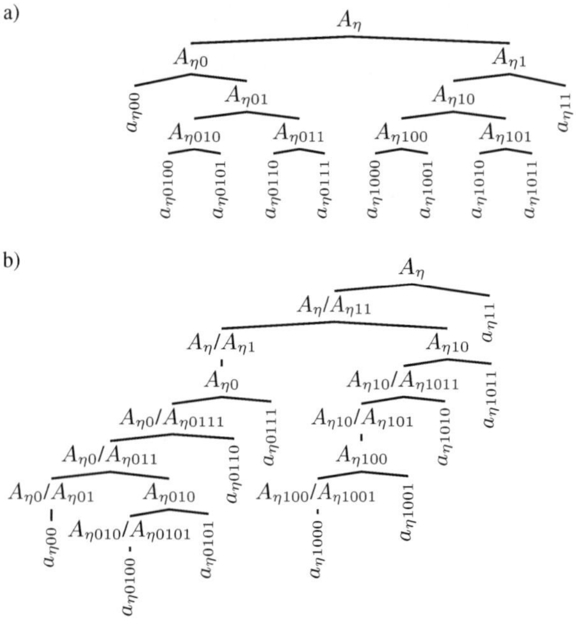

Figure 1: Sample right-corner transform of schematized tree before (a) and after (b) application of transform.

is mapped to the top of a left-expanding sequence in a right-corner transformed tree:

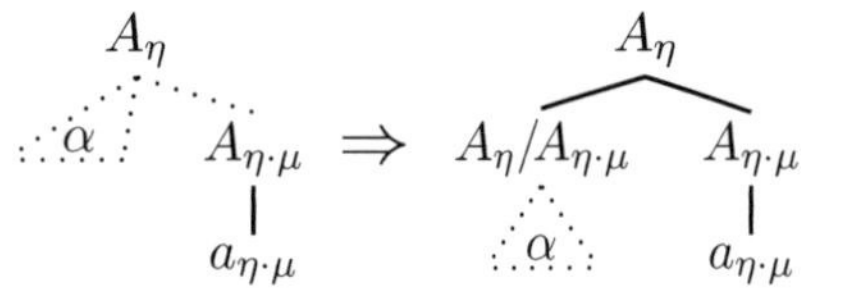

(3)

The application of this transform is exemplified in Figure 1.

3.2 Hierarchical Hidden Markov Models

Right-corner transformed trees are mapped to random variables in a Hierarchical Hidden Markov Model (Murphy and Paskin, 2001).

A Hierarchical Hidden Markov Model (HHMM) is essentially a factored version of a Hidden Markov Model (HMM), configured to recognize bounded recursive structures (i.e. trees). Like HMMs, HHMMs use Viterbi decoding to obtain sequences of hidden states $\hat{s}_{1..T}$ given sequences of observations $o_{1..T}$ (words or audio features), through independence assumptions in a transition model Θ_A and an observation model Θ_B (Baker, 1975; Jelinek et al., 1975):

$$\hat{s}_{1..T} \overset{\text{def}}{=} \underset{s_{1..T}}{\text{argmax}} \prod_{t=1}^{T} \mathsf{P}_{\Theta_A}(s_t \mid s_{t-1}) \cdot \mathsf{P}_{\Theta_B}(o_t \mid s_t) \tag{4}$$

HHMMs then factor the hidden state transition Θ_A into a reduce and shift phase (Equation 5), then into a bounded set of depth-specific operations (Equation 6):

$$\mathsf{P}_{\Theta_A}(s_t|s_{t-1}) = \sum_{r_t} \mathsf{P}_{\Theta_R}(r_t|s_{t-1}) \cdot \mathsf{P}_{\Theta_S}(s_t|r_t\, s_{t-1}) \tag{5}$$

$$\overset{\text{def}}{=} \sum_{r_t^{1..D}} \prod_{d=1}^{D} \mathsf{P}_{\Theta_{R,d}}(r_t^d \mid r_t^{d+1}\, s_{t-1}^d\, s_{t-1}^{d-1}) \cdot \mathsf{P}_{\Theta_{S,d}}(s_t^d \mid r_t^{d+1}\, r_t^d\ s_{t-1}^d\, s_t^{d-1}) \tag{6}$$

which allow depth-specific variables to reduce (through $\Theta_{\text{R-Rdn},d}$), transition ($\Theta_{\text{S-Trn},d}$), and expand ($\Theta_{\text{S-Exp},d}$) like tape symbols in a pushdown automaton with a bounded memory store, depending on whether the variable below has reduced ($r_t^d \in R_G$) or not ($r_t^d \notin R_G$):[2]

$$\mathsf{P}_{\Theta_{R,d}}(r_t^d \mid r_t^{d+1}\, s_{t-1}^d\, s_{t-1}^{d-1}) \overset{\text{def}}{=} \begin{cases} \text{if } r_t^{d+1} \notin R_G : [\![r_t^d = \mathbf{r}_\top]\!] \\ \text{if } r_t^{d+1} \in R_G : \mathsf{P}_{\Theta_{\text{R-Rdn},d}}(r_t^d \mid r_t^{d+1}\ s_{t-1}^d\ s_{t-1}^{d-1}) \end{cases} \tag{7}$$

$$\mathsf{P}_{\Theta_{S,d}}(s_t^d \mid r_t^{d+1} r_t^d\ s_{t-1}^d\, s_t^{d-1}) \overset{\text{def}}{=} \begin{cases} \text{if } r_t^{d+1} \notin R_G,\ r_t^d \notin R_G : [\![s_t^d = s_{t-1}^d]\!] \\ \text{if } r_t^{d+1} \in R_G,\ r_t^d \notin R_G : \mathsf{P}_{\Theta_{\text{S-Trn},d}}(s_t^d \mid r_t^{d+1} r_t^d\ s_{t-1}^d\, s_t^{d-1}) \\ \text{if } r_t^{d+1} \in R_G,\ r_t^d \in R_G : \mathsf{P}_{\Theta_{\text{S-Exp},d}}(s_t^d \mid s_t^{d-1}) \end{cases} \tag{8}$$

where $s_t^0 = \mathbf{s}_\top$ and $r_t^{D+1} = \mathbf{r}_\bot$ for constants $\mathbf{s}_\top$ (an incomplete root constituent), $\mathbf{r}_\bot$ (a complete lexical constituent) and $\mathbf{r}_\top$ (a null state resulting from reduction failure) s.t. $\mathbf{r}_\bot \in R_G$ and $\mathbf{r}_\top \notin R_G$.

Right-corner transformed trees, as exemplified in Figure 1(b), can then be aligned to HHMM states as shown in Figure 2, and used to train an HHMM as a parser.

Parsing with an HHMM simply involves processing the input sequence, and estimating a most likely hidden state sequence given this observed input. Since the output is to be the best possible parse, the Viterbi algorithm is used, which keeps track of the highest probability state at each time step, where the state is the store of incomplete syntactic constituents being processed. State transitions are computed using the models above, and each state at each time step keeps a back pointer to the state it most probably came from. Extracting the highest probability parse requires extracting

[2] Here, $[\![\cdot]\!]$ is an indicator function: $[\![\phi]\!] = 1$ if ϕ is true, 0 otherwise.

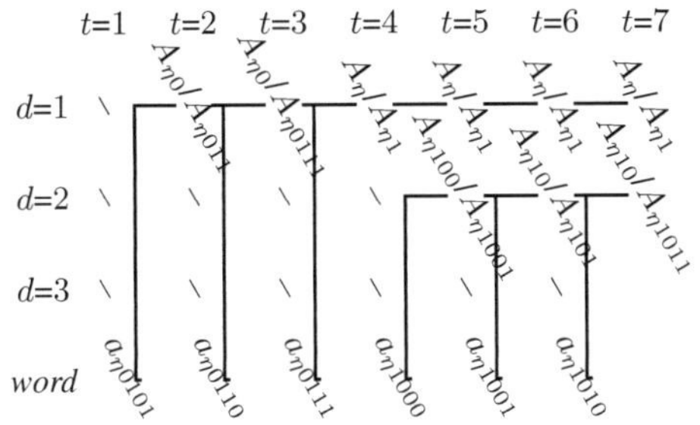

Figure 2: Mapping of schematized right-corner tree into HHMM memory elements.

the most likely sequence, deterministically mapping that sequence back to a right-corner tree, and reversing the right-corner transform to produce an ordinary phrase structure tree.

Unfortunately exact inference is not tractable with this model and dataset. The state space is too large to manage for both space and time reasons, and thus approximate inference is carried out, through the use of a beam search. At each time step, only the top N most probable hypothesized states are maintained. Experiments described in (Schuler, 2009) suggest that there does not seem to be much lost in going from exact inference using the CKY algorithm to a beam search with a relatively large width. However, the opposite experiment, examining the effect of going from a relatively wide beam to a very narrow beam has not been thoroughly studied in this parsing architecture.

4 Optionally Arc-eager Parsing

The right-corner transform described in Section 3.1 saves memory because it transforms any right-expanding sequence with left-child subtrees into a left-expanding sequence of incomplete constituents, with the same sequence of subtrees as right children. The left-branching sequences of siblings resulting from this transform can then be composed bottom-up through time by replacing each left child category with the category of the resulting parent, within the same memory element (or depth level). For example, in Figure 3(a) a left-child category NP/NP at time t=4 is composed with a noun *new* of category NP/NNP (a noun phrase lacking a proper noun yet to come), resulting in a new parent category NP/NNP at time t=5 replacing the left child category NP/NP in the topmost d=1 memory element.

This in-element composition preserves elements of the bounded memory store for use in processing descendants of this composed constituent, yielding the human-like memory demands reported in (Schuler et al., 2008). But whenever an in-element composition like this is hypothesized, it isolates an intermediate constituent (in this example, the noun phrase 'new york city') from subsequent composition. Allowing access to this intermediate constituent — for example, to allow 'new york city' to become a modifier of 'bonds', which itself becomes an argument of 'for' — requires an analysis in which the intermediate constituent is stored in a separate memory element, shown in Figure 3(b). This creates a local ambiguity in the parser (in this case, from time step t=4) that may have to be propagated across several words before it can be resolved (in this case, at time step t=7). This is essentially an ambiguity between arc-eager (in-element) and arc-standard (cross-element) composition strategies, as described by Abney and Johnson (1991). In contrast, an ordinary (purely arc-standard) parser with an unbounded stack would only hypothesize analysis (b), avoiding this ambiguity.[3]

The right-corner HHMM approach described in this paper relies on a learned statistical model to predict when in-element (arc-eager) compositions will occur, in addition to hypothesizing parse trees. The model encodes a mixed strategy: with some probability arc-eager or arc-standard for each possible expansion. Accuracy results on a right-corner HHMM model trained on the Penn Wall Street Journal Treebank suggest that this kind of optionally arc-eager strategy can be reliably statistically learned.

By placing firm limits on the number of open incomplete constituents in working memory, the Hierarchical HMM parser maintains parallel hypotheses on the beam which predict whether each constituent will host a subsequent attachment or not. Empirical results described in the next section

[3]It is important to note that neither the right-corner nor left-corner parsing strategy by itself creates this ambiguity. The ambiguity arises from the decision to use this optionally arc-eager strategy to reduce memory store allocation in a bounded memory parser. Implementations of left-corner parsers such as that of Henderson (2004) adopt a arc-standard strategy, essentially always choosing analysis (b) above, and thus do not introduce this kind of local ambiguity. But in adopting this strategy, such parsers must maintain a stack memory of unbounded size, and thus are not attractive as models of human parsing in short-term memory (Resnik, 1992).

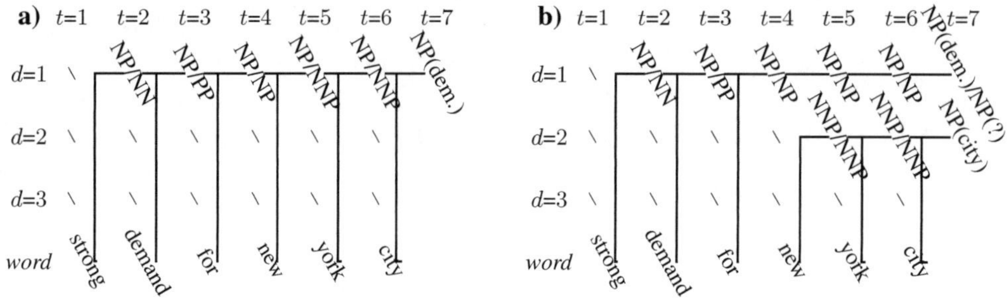

Figure 3: Alternative analyses of 'strong demand for new york city ...': a) using in-element composition, compatible with 'strong demand for new york city is ...' (in which the demand is for the city); and b) using cross-element (or delayed) composition, compatible with either 'strong demand for new york city is ...' (in which the demand is for the city) or 'strong demand for new york city bonds is ...' (in which a forthcoming referent — in this case, bonds — is associated with the city, and is in demand). In-element composition (a) saves memory but closes off access to the noun phrase headed by 'city', and so is not incompatible with the '...bonds' completion. Cross-element composition (b) requires more memory, but allows access to the noun phrase headed by 'city', so is compatible with either completion. This ambiguity is introduced at t=4 and propagated until at least t=7. An ordinary, non-right-corner stack machine would exclusively use analysis (b), avoiding ambiguity.

show that this added demand on parallelism does not substantially degrade parsing accuracy, even at very narrow beam widths.

5 Experimental Evaluation

The parsing model described in Section 3 has previously been evaluated on the standard task of parsing the Wall Street Journal section of the Penn Treebank. This evaluation was optimized for accuracy results, and reported a relatively wide beam width of 2000 to achieve its best results. However, most psycholinguistic models of the human sentence processing mechanism suggest that if the HSPM does work in parallel, it does so with a much lower number of concurrent hypotheses (Boston et al., 2008b). Viewing the HHMM parsing framework as a psycholinguistic model, a necessary (though not sufficient) condition for it being a valid model is that it be able to maintain relatively accurate parsing capabilities even at much lower beam widths.

Thus, the first experiments in this paper evaluate the degradation of parsing accuracy depending on beam width of the HHMM parser. Experiments were conducted again on the WSJ Penn Treebank, using sections 02-21 to train, and section 23 as the test set. Punctuation was included in both training and testing. A set of varied beam widths were considered, from a high of 2000 to a low of 15. This range was meant to roughly correspond to the range of parallelism used in other similar experiments, using 2000 as a high end due to its usage in previous parsing experiments. However, it should be noted that in fact the highest value of 2000 is already an approximate search – preliminary experiments showed that exhaustive search with the HHMM would require more than 100000 elements per time step (exact values may be much higher but could not be collected because they exhausted system memory).

The HHMM parser was compared to a custom built (though standard) probabilistic CKY parser implementation trained on the CNF trees used as input to the right-corner transform, so that the CKY parser was able to compete on a fair footing. The accuracy results of these experiments are shown in Figure 4.

These results show fairly graceful decline in parsing accuracy with a beam width starting at 2000 elements down to about 50 beam elements. This beam width is much less than 1% of the exhaustive search, though it is around 1% of what might be considered the highest reasonable beam width for efficient parsing. The lowest beam widths attempted, 15, 20, and 25, result in accuracy below that of the CKY parser. The lowest beam width attempted, 15, shows the sharpest decline in accuracy, putting the HHMM system nearly 8 points below the CKY parser in terms of accuracy.

This compares reasonably well to results by

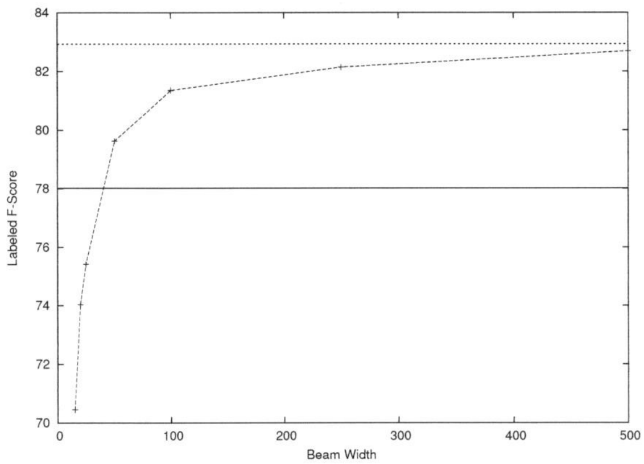

Figure 4: Plot of parsing accuracy (labeled F-score) vs. beam widths for an HHMM parser (curved line). Top line is HHMM accuracy with beam width of 2000 (upper bound). The bottom line is CKY parser results. Points correspond to beam widths of 15, 20, 25, 50, 100, 250, and 500.

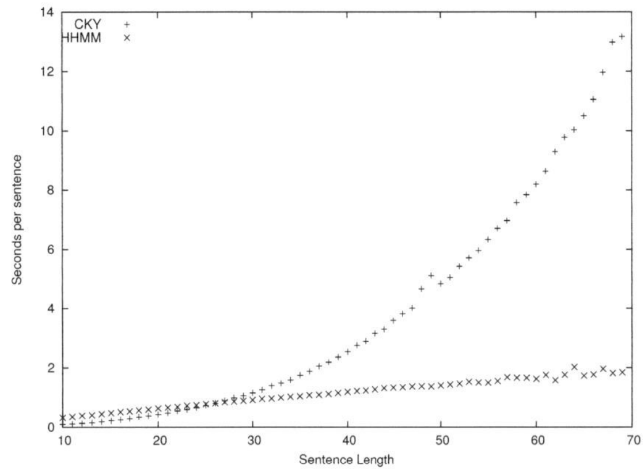

Figure 5: Plot of parsing time vs. sentence length for HHMM and CKY parsers.

Brants and Crocker (2000) showing that an incremental chart-parsing algorithm can parse accurately with pruning down to 1% of normal memory usage. While that parsing algorithm is difficult to compare directly to this HHMM parser, the reduction in beam width in this system to 50 beam elements from an already approximated 2000 beam elements shows similar robustness to approximation. Accuracy comparisons should be taken with a grain of salt due to additional annotations performed to the Treebank before training, but the HHMM parser with a beam width of 50 obtains approximately the same accuracy as the Brants and Crocker incremental CKY parser pruning to 3% of chart size. At 1% pruning, Brants and Crocker achieved around 75% accuracy, which falls between the HHMM parser at beam widths of 20 and 25.

Results by Boston et al. (2008b) are also difficult to compare directly due to a difference in parsing algorithm and different research priority (that paper was attempting to correlate parsing difficulty with reading difficulty). However, that paper showed that a dependency parser using less than ten beam elements (and as few as one) was just as capable of predicting reading difficulty as the parser using 100 beam elements.

A second experiment was conducted to evaluate the HHMM for its time efficiency in parsing. This experiment is intended to address two questions: Whether this framework is efficient enough to be considered a viable psycholinguistic model, and whether its parsing time and accuracy remain competitive with more standard cubic time parsing technologies at low beam widths. To evaluate this aspect, the HHMM parser was run at low beam widths on sentences of varying lengths. The baseline was the widely-used Stanford parser (Klein and Manning, 2003), run in 'vanilla PCFG' mode. This parser was used rather than the custom-built CKY parser from the previous experiment, to avoid the possibility that its implementation was not efficient enough to provide a realistic test. The HHMM parser was implemented as described in the previous section. These experiments were run on a machine with a single 2.40 GHz Celeron CPU, with 512 MB of RAM. In both implementations the parser timing includes only time spent actually parsing sentences, ignoring the overhead incurred by reading in model files or training.

Figure 5 shows a plot of parsing time versus sentence length for the HHMM parser for a beam width of 20. Sentences shorter than 10 words were not included for visual clarity (both parsers are extremely fast at that length). At this beam width, the performance of the HHMM parser (labeled F-score) was 74.03%, compared to 71% for a plain CKY parser. As expected, the HHMM parsing time increases linearly with sentence length, while the CKY parsing time increases super-linearly. (However, due to high constants in the run time complexity of the HHMM, it was not a priori clear that the HHMM would be faster for any sentence of reasonable length.)

The results of this experiment show that the HHMM parser is indeed competitive with a probabilistic CKY parser, in terms of parsing efficiency, even while parsing with higher accuracy. At sentences longer that 26 words (including punctuation), the HHMM parser is faster than the CKY parser. This advantage is clear for segmented text such as the Wall Street Journal corpus. However, this advantage is compounded when considering unsegmented or ambiguously segmented text such as transcribed speech or less formal written text, as the HHMM parser can also make decisions about where to put sentence breaks, and do so in linear time.[4]

6 Conclusion and Future Work

This paper furthers the case for the HHMM as a viable psycholinguistic model of the human parsing mechanism by showing that performance degrades gracefully as parallelism decreases, providing reasonably accurate parsing even at very low beam widths. In addition, this work shows that an HHMM parser run at low beam widths is competitive in speed with parsers that don't work incrementally, because of its asymptotically linear runtime.

This is especially surprising given that the HHMM uses parallel hypotheses on the beam to predict whether constituents will remain open for attachment or not. Success at low beam widths suggests that this optionally arc-eager prediction is something that is indeed relatively predictable during parsing, lending credence to claims of psycholinguistic relevance of HHMM parsing.

Future work should explore further directions in improving parsing performance at low beam widths. The lowest beam value experiments presented here generally parsed fairly accurately when they completed, but were already encountering problems with unparseable sentences that negatively affected parser accuracy. The large accuracy decrease between beam sizes of 20 and 15 is likely to be mostly due to the lack of any correct analysis on the beam when the sentence is completed.

It should be noted, however, that no adjustments were made to the parser's syntactic model with these beam variations. This syntactic model was optimized for accuracy at the standard beam width of 2000, and thus contains some state splittings that are beneficial at wide beam widths, but at low beam widths are redundant and prevent otherwise valid hypotheses from being maintained on the beam. For applications in which speed is a priority, future research can evaluate tradeoffs in accuracy that occur at different beam widths with a coarser-grained syntactic representation that allows for more variation of hypotheses even on very small beams.

[4]It does this probabilistically as a side effect of the parsing, by choosing an analysis in which $r_t^0 \in R_G$ (for any t).

Acknowledgments

This research was supported by National Science Foundation CAREER/PECASE award 0447685. The views expressed are not necessarily endorsed by the sponsors.

References

Steven P. Abney and Mark Johnson. 1991. Memory requirements and local ambiguities of parsing strategies. *J. Psycholinguistic Research*, 20(3):233–250.

James Baker. 1975. The Dragon system: an overivew. *IEEE Transactions on Acoustics, Speech and Signal Processing*, 23(1):24–29.

Thomas G. Bever. 1970. The cognitive basis for linguistic structure. In J.Ř. Hayes, editor, *Cognition and the Development of Language*, pages 279–362. Wiley, New York.

Marisa Ferrara Boston, John T. Hale, Reinhold Kliegl, Umesh Patil, and Shravan Vasishth. 2008a. Parsing costs as predictors of reading difficulty: An evaluation using the Potsdam Sentence Corpus. *Journal of Eye Movement Research*, 2(1):1–12.

Marisa Ferrara Boston, John T. Hale, Reinhold Kliegl, and Shravan Vasishth. 2008b. Surprising parser actions and reading difficulty. In *Proceedings of ACL-08: HLT, Short Papers*, pages 5–8, Columbus, Ohio, June. Association for Computational Linguistics.

Thorsten Brants and Matthew Crocker. 2000. Probabilistic parsing and psychological plausibility. In *Proceedings of COLING '00*, pages 111–118.

Noam Chomsky and George A. Miller. 1963. Introduction to the formal analysis of natural languages. In *Handbook of Mathematical Psychology*, pages 269–321. Wiley.

Nelson Cowan. 2001. The magical number 4 in short-term memory: A reconsideration of mental storage capacity. *Behavioral and Brain Sciences*, 24:87–185.

Matthew Crocker and Thorsten Brants. 2000. Wide-coverage probabilistic sentence processing. *Journal of Psycholinguistic Research*, 29(6):647–669.

John Hale. 2001. A probabilistic earley parser as a psycholinguistic model. In *Proceedings of the Second Meeting of the North American Chapter of the Association for Computational Linguistics*, pages 159–166, Pittsburgh, PA.

James Henderson. 2004. Lookahead in deterministic left-corner parsing. In *Proc. Workshop on Incremental Parsing: Bringing Engineering and Cognition Together*, pages 26–33, Barcelona, Spain.

Frederick Jelinek, Lalit R. Bahl, and Robert L. Mercer. 1975. Design of a linguistic statistical decoder for the recognition of continuous speech. *IEEE Transactions on Information Theory*, 21:250–256.

Dan Klein and Christopher D. Manning. 2003. Accurate unlexicalized parsing. In *Proceedings of the 41st Annual Meeting of the Association for Computational Linguistics*, pages 423–430, Sapporo, Japan.

Richard L. Lewis. 2000. Falsifying serial and parallel parsing models: Empirical conundrums and an overlooked paradigm. *Journal of Psycholinguistic Research*, 29:241–248.

Mitchell P. Marcus, Beatrice Santorini, and Mary Ann Marcinkiewicz. 1993. Building a large annotated corpus of English: the Penn Treebank. *Computational Linguistics*, 19(2):313–330.

George A. Miller. 1956. The magical number seven, plus or minus two: Some limits on our capacity for processing information. *Psychological Review*, 63:81–97.

Kevin P. Murphy and Mark A. Paskin. 2001. Linear time inference in hierarchical HMMs. In *Proc. NIPS*, pages 833–840, Vancouver, BC, Canada.

Philip Resnik. 1992. Left-corner parsing and psychological plausibility. In *Proceedings of COLING*, pages 191–197, Nantes, France.

Brian Roark, Asaf Bachrach, Carlos Cardenas, and Christophe Pallier. 2009. Deriving lexical and syntactic expectation-based measures for psycholinguistic modeling via incremental top-down parsing. *Proceedings of the 2009 Conference on Empirical Methods in Natural Langauge Processing*, pages 324–333.

William Schuler, Samir AbdelRahman, Tim Miller, and Lane Schwartz. 2008. Toward a psycholinguistically-motivated model of language. In *Proceedings of COLING*, pages 785–792, Manchester, UK, August.

William Schuler, Samir AbdelRahman, Tim Miller, and Lane Schwartz. 2010. Broad-coverage incremental parsing using human-like memory constraints. *Computational Linguistics*, 36(1).

William Schuler. 2009. Parsing with a bounded stack using a model-based right-corner transform. In *Proceedings of the North American Association for Computational Linguistics (NAACL '09)*, pages 344–352, Boulder, Colorado.

Stephen Wu, Asaf Bachrach, Carlos Cardenas, and William Schuler. 2010. Complexity metrics in an incremental right-corner parser. In *Proceedings of the 49th Annual Conference of the Association for Computational Linguistics*.

The role of memory in superiority violation gradience

Marisa Ferrara Boston
Cornell University
Ithaca, NY, USA
mfb74@cornell.edu

Abstract

This paper examines how grammatical and memory constraints explain gradience in superiority violation acceptability. A computational model encoding both categories of constraints is compared to experimental evidence. By formalizing memory capacity as beam-search in the parser, the model predicts gradience evident in human data. To predict attachment behavior, the parser must be sensitive to the types of nominal intervenors that occur between a wh-filler and its head. The results suggest memory is more informative for modeling violation gradience patterns than grammatical constraints.

1 Introduction

Sentences that include two wh-words, as in Example (1), are often considered difficult by English speakers.

(1) *Diego asked **what**$_1$ *who*$_2$ read?

This superiority effect holds when a second wh-word, who in this example, acts as a barrier to attachment of the first wh-word and its verb (Chomsky, 1973).

The difficulty is ameliorated when the wh-words are switched to *which-N*, or which-Noun, form as in Examples (2) and (3) (Karttunen, 1977; Pesetsky, 1987). This is confirmed by experimental evidence (Arnon et al., To appear; Hofmeister, 2007).

(2) ?Diego asked **which book** *who* read?

(3) ?Diego asked **what** *which girl* read?

Memory is often implicated as the source of this gradience, though it is unclear which aspects of memory best model experimental results. This computational model encodes grammatical and memory-based constraints proposed in the literature to account for the phenomenon. The results demonstrate that as memory resources are increased, the parser can model the human pattern if it is sensitive to the types of nominal intervenors. This supports memory-based accounts of superiority violation (SUV) gradience.

2 Explanations for SUV gradience

This section details grammatical and reductionist explanations for SUV gradience, motivating the encoding of various constraints in the computational model.

2.1 Grammatical explanations

Grammatical accounts of gradience rely on intrinsic discourse differences between phrases that allow for SUVs and those that do not. In this work, which-N phrases are examples of the former, and so-called bare wh-phrases (including who and $what$) the latter[1]. Rizzi (1990) incorporates ideas from Pesetsky's D-Linking, or $discourse$-linking, hypothesis (1987) into a grammatical account of SUV gradience, Relativized Minimality. He argues that $referential$ phrases like *which-N* refer to a pre-established set in the discourse and are not subject to the same constraints on attachment as *non-referential* phrases, like $what$. *Which book* delimits a set of possible discourse entities, *books*, and is more restrictive than $what$, which could instead delimit sets of books, cats, or abstract entities. The Relativized Minimality hypothesis accounts for SUV gradience on the basis of this categorical separation on wh-phrases in the discourse.

[1] Both bare phrases and which-N phrases could have the appropriate discourse conditions to allow for superiority violations, and vice versa. However, to relate the theory's predictions to the experiment modeled here, I use a categorical split between which-N and bare wh-phrases.

Proceedings of the 2010 Workshop on Cognitive Modeling and Computational Linguistics, ACL 2010, pages 36–44,
Uppsala, Sweden, 15 July 2010.

2.2 Reductionist explanations

Many grammatical accounts, particularly those that are grounded in cognitive factors, incorporate some element of processing or memory in their explanations (Phillips, Submitted). Reductionist accounts are different; their proponents do not believe that superiority requires a grammatical explanation. Rather, SUVs that appear ungrammatical, such as Example (1), are the result of severe processing difficulty alone.

These accounts attribute processing difficulty to memory: severe memory resource limitations account for ungrammatical sentences in SUVs, and increased memory resources allow for more acceptable sentences. This is the central idea behind Hofmeister's Memory Facilitation Hypothesis (2007):

> **Memory Facilitation Hypothesis**
> Linguistic elements that encode more information (lexical, semantic, syntactic, etc.) facilitate their own subsequent retrieval from memory (Hofmeister, 2007, p.4)[2].

This memory explanation is central to activation-based memory hypotheses previously proposed in the psycholinguistic literature, such as CC-READER (Just and Carpenter, 1992), ACT-R (Lewis and Vasishth, 2005), and 4CAPS (Just and Varma, 2007). This work considers activation, and manipulates memory resources by varying the number of analyses the parser considers at each parse step.

Table 1 lists memory factors that may contribute to SUV gradience. They are sensitive to the memory resources available during syntactic parsing, but account for memory differently. Below I describe these variations.

2.2.1 Distance and the DLT

Distance, as measured by the number of words between, for example, a *wh*-word and its verb, has been argued to affect sentence comprehension (Wanner and Maratsos, 1978; Rambow and Joshi, 1994; Gibson, 1998). Experimental evidence supports this claim, but there exist a number of anomalous results that resist explanation in terms of distance alone (Gibson, 1998; Hawkins, 1999; Gibson, 2000). For example, it is not the case that processing difficulty increases solely as a function of the number of words in a sentence. However, it is possible that SUV gradience could be affected by this simple metric.

The Dependency Locality Theory (DLT) (Gibson, 2000) is a more linguistically-informed measure of distance. The DLT argues that an accurate model of sentence processing difficulty is sensitive to the number and discourse-status (given or new) of nominal intervenors that occur across a particular distance. The DLT's sensitivity to discourse-newness integrates aspects of D-linking: *which book*, for example, requires that books already be a part of the discourse, though *what* does not (Gundel et al., 1993; Warren and Gibson, 2002). The DLT has been demonstrated to model difficulty in ways that simple distance alone can not (Grodner and Gibson, 2005).

This study also considers a stronger version of the DLT, Intervenors. Intervenors considers both the number and part-of-speech (POS) of nominal intervenors between a *wh*-word and its head. This feature is sensitive to nuanced differences between nominal intervenors, providing a more accurate model of the Memory Facilitation Hypothesis.

2.2.2 Stack memory

Distance can also be measured in terms of the parser's internal resources. The computational model described here incorporates a stack memory. Although stacks are not accurate models of human memory (McElree, 2000), this architectural property may provide insight into how memory affects SUV gradience.

2.2.3 Activation and interference

Sentence processing difficulty has been attributed to the amount of time it takes to retrieve a word from memory. Lewis & Vasishth (2005) find support for this argument by applying equations from a general cognitive model, ACT-R (Adaptive Control of Thought-Rational) (Anderson, 2005), to a sentence processsing model. Their calculation of retrieval time, henceforth retrieval, is sensitive to a word's activation and its similarity-based interference with other words in memory (Gordon et al., 2002; Van Dyke and McElree, 2006). Activation, Interference, and the conjunction of the two in the form of Retrieval, are considered in this work.

The grammatical and memory-based accounts described above offer several explanations for SUV gradience. They can be represented along a continuum, where the type of information consid-

[2]Recent work by Hofmeister and colleagues attributes the advantage to a decrease in memory interference rather than retrieval facilitation (Submitted), but the spirit of the work remains the same.

Hypothesis	Sensitive to
Distance	String distance between words.
DLT	Number of nominal intervenors.
Intervenors	POS of nominal intervenors.
Stack Memory	Elements currently in parser memory.
Baseline Activation	Amount structure is activated in memory.
Interference	Amount of competition from similar words in memory.
Retrieval	Retrieval time of word from memory.

Table 1: Memory-based sentence processing theories.

ered in memory varies from the simple (Distance) to complex (Retrieval), as in (4).

(4) Distance < DLT < Intervenors < Stack Memory < Activation < Interference < Retrieval

Despite this representation, in this work I consider each as an independent theory. Together, they form the hypothesis set in the model, selected because they represent the major explanations posited for gradience in SUVs and related phenomena, like islands.

The computational model not only formalizes the memory accounts, but also provides a framework for memory-based factors that require a computational model, such as retrieval. The results determine memory factors that best account for SUV gradience patterns.

3 Methodology

The test set for SUV gradience is the experimental results from Arnon et al. (To appear). The experiment tests gradience across four conditions, shown in Examples (5)-(8).

(5) Pat wondered **what** *who* read. (bare.bare)

(6) Pat wondered **what** *which student* read. (bare.which)

(7) Pat wondered **which book** *who* read. (which.bare)

(8) Pat wondered **which book** *which student* read. (which.which)

The conditions substitute the wh-type of both **wh-fillers** and *wh-intervenors* in the island context. In Example (5) both the filler and intervenor are bare (the bare.bare condition), whereas in Example (8), both the filler and intervenor are which-Ns (which.which). Examples (6) and (7) provide the other possible configurations.

Arnon and colleagues find which.which to be the fastest condition. Figure 1 depicts these results. The other conditions are more difficult,

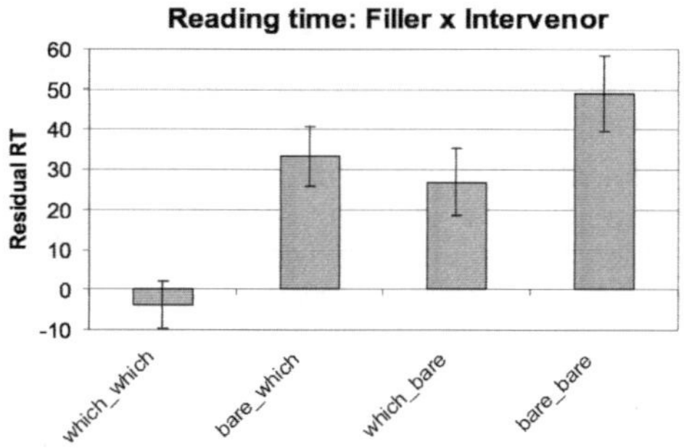

Figure 1: Reading time is fastest in the which.which condition (Arnon et al., To appear, p.5).

at varying levels: the which.bare condition is less difficult than the bare.which condition, and both are less difficult than the bare.bare condition. These results roughly pattern with acceptability judgments discussed in syntactic literature (Pesetsky, 1987).

Corpora for superiority processing results do not exist. Further, few studies on SUVs incorporate the same structures, techniques, and experimental conditions. Although Arnon et al. considered 20 lexical variations, the unlexicalized parser can not distinguish these variations. Therefore, the parser is only evaluated on these four sentences; however, they are taken to represent classes of structures that generalize to all SUV gradience in English.

3.1 The parsing model

The computational model is based on Nivre's (2004) dependency parsing algorithm. The algorithm builds directed, word-to-word analyses of test input following the Dependency Grammar syntactic formalism (Tesnière, 1959; Hays, 1964). Figure 2 depicts the full dependency analysis of the which.which condition from Example

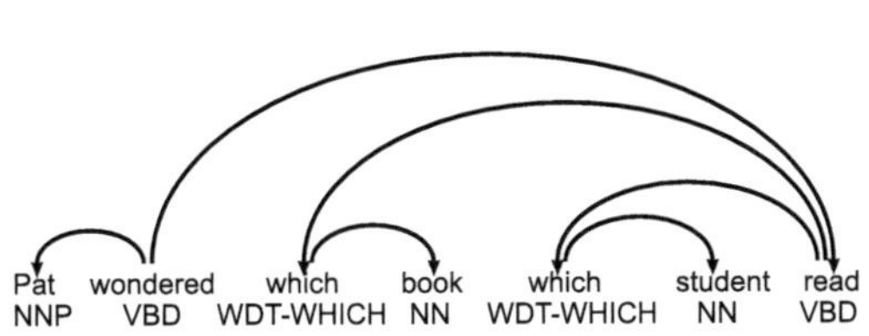

Figure 2: A dependency analysis of the which.which condition.

(8), where *heads* point to their *dependents* via arcs.

The Nivre parser assembles dependency structure incrementally by passing through parser states that aggregate four data structures, shown in Table 2. The stack σ holds parsed words that require further analysis, and the list τ holds words yet to be parsed. h and d encode the current list of dependency relations.

σ	A stack of already-parsed unreduced words.
τ	An ordered input list of words.
h	A function from dependent words to heads.
d	A function from dependent words to arc types.

Table 2: Parser configuration.

The parser transitions from state to state via four possible actions. `Shift` and `Reduce` manipulate σ. `LeftArc` and `RightArc` build dependencies between σ_1 (the element at the top of the stack) and τ_1 (the next input word); `LeftArc` makes σ_1 the dependent, and `RightArc` makes σ_1 the head.

The parser determines actions by consulting a probability model derived from the Brown Corpus (Francis and Kucera, 1979). The corpus is converted to dependencies via the Pennconverter tool (Johansson and Nugues, 2007). The parser is then simulated on these dependencies, providing a corpus of parser states and subsequent actions that form the basis of the training data. Because the parser is POS-based, this corpus is manipulated in two ways to sensitize it to the differences in the experimental conditions. First, the corpus is given finer-grained POS tags for each of the wh-words, described in Table 3.

Secondly, *which-N* dependencies are encoded as DPs (determiner phrases) and are headed by the wh-phrase (Abney, 1987). This ensures the parser differentiates a wh-word retrieval from a simple $noun$ retrieval, which is necessary for several of the memory-based constraints. Other noun phrases are headed by their nouns. The corpus is not switched to a fully DP analysis to preserve as many of the original relationships as possible.

Original POS	*Wh*	Example
WP	WP-WHAT	what
WP	WP-WHO	who
WDT	WDT-WHICH	*which* book
WDT	WDT-WHAT	*what* book
IN	IN-WHETHER	*whether*
WRB	WRB	how/why/when

Table 3: POS for *wh* fillers and intervenors.

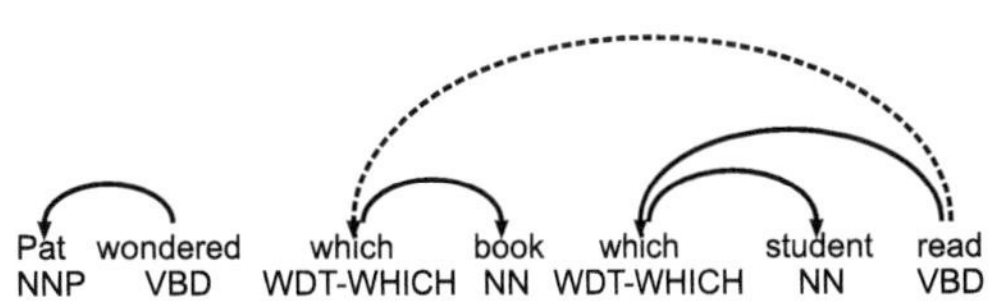

Figure 3: The relevant attachment is between *which* and *read*.

I extend the Nivre algorithm to allow for beam search within the parser state space. This allows the parser to consider different degrees of parallelism k, and manipulate the amount of memory allotted to incremental parse states. This manipulation serves as a model of variation in an individual's memory as a sentence is parsed.

3.2 Evaluation

To determine how well the accounts model the experimental data, I consider the likelihood of the parser resolving the island-violating dependency between wh-fillers and their verbs in the Arnon et al. data. In terms of the dependency parser, the test determines whether the parser creates a `LeftArc` attachment in a state where $which$ or $what$ is σ_1 and $read$ is τ_1. The dependency structure associated with this parser state is depicted in Figure 3 for the which.which condition.

This evaluation is categorical rather than statistical: SUV-processing is based on the decision to form an attachment in a superiority-violating context, given four experimental sentences. While future work will incorporate more experiments for robust statistical analysis, this work focuses on a small subset that generalizes to the greater phenomenon.

3.3 Encoding constraints

The parser determines actions on the basis of probabilistic models, or $features$. In this work, I encode each of the grammatical and memory-based explanations as its own feature. I normalize the weights from the LIBLINEAR (Lin et al., 2008) SVM classification tool to determine probabilities for each parser action (`LeftArc, RightArc, Shift, Reduce`). The features are sensitive to specific aspects of the current parser state, allowing an examination of whether the features suggest the superiority violating `LeftArc` action in the context depicted in Figure 3. The prediction is that attachment will be easiest in the which.which condition and impossible in the other conditions when memory resources are limited (k=1), as in Table 4.

Condition	b.b	b.w	w.b	w.w
Attachment	N	N	N	Y

Table 4: `LeftArc` attachments given Arnon et al. (To appear) results. **Y** = Yes, **N**=No.

Table 5 depicts the full list of grammatical and memory-based features considered in this study, which are detailed below.

3.3.1 Grammatical constraint

In Relativized Minimality, referential noun phrases override superiority violations, whereas non-referential noun phrases do not. This constraint is included as a probabilistic feature of the parser, RELMIN, specified in Table 5. The condition holds if a non-referential NP ($what$) is in σ_1 (RELMIN=Yes). But the violation condition does not hold (RELMIN=No) if a non-referential NP (*which*) is in σ_1. The feature categorically separates which-N and bare wh-phrases to capture the Relativized Minimality predictions for these experimental sentences. The probabilistic feature also adds a grammatical gradience component to the model, which is not proposed by the original hypothesis.

3.3.2 Memory constraints

The parser encodes each of the memory accounts provided in Table 1 as probabilistic features. DISTANCE, the simplest feature, determines parser actions on the basis of how far apart σ_1 and τ_1 are in the string.

DLT and INTERVENORS require parser sensitivity to the nominal intervenors between σ_1 and τ_1 according to Gibson's DLT specification (2000). Table 6 provides a list of the nominal intervenors considered. Gibson's hierarchy is extended to include nominal wh-words to more accurately model the experimental conditions.

Intervenor POS	Example
NN	book
NNS	books
PRP	they
NNP	Pat
NNPS	Americans
WP-WHAT	what
WP-WHO	who
WDT-WHICH	*which* book
WDT-WHAT	*what* book

Table 6: POS for nominal intervenors.

The sequence of STACKNEXT features are sensitive to the parser's memory, in the form of the POS of elements at varying depths of the stack. These features are found to have high overall accuracy in the Nivre parser (Nivre, 2004) and in human sentence processing modeling (Boston et al., 2008).

ACTIVATION, INTERFERENCE, and RETRIEVAL predictions are based on the sequence of Lewis & Vasisth (2005) calculations provided in Equations 1-4. These equations require some notion of duration, which is calculated as a function of parser actions and word retrieval times. Table 7 describes this calculation, motivated by the production rule time in Lewis & Vasisth's ACT-R model.

Transition	Time
LEFT	50 ms + 50 ms + Retrieval Time
RIGHT	50 ms + 50 ms + Retrieval Time
SHIFT	50ms
REDUCE	0ms

Table 7: How time is determined in the parser.

Because only words at the top of the stack can be retrieved, the following will be described for σ_1. Retrieval time for σ_1 is based on its activation A, calculated as in Equation 1.

$$A_i = B_i + \sum_j W_j S_{ji} \quad (1)$$

Total activation is the sum of two quantities, the word's baseline activation B_i and similarity-based interference for that word, calculated in the second addend of the equation. The baseline activation, provided in Equation 2, increases with more

Feature	Feature Type	Includes
Grammar		
RELMIN	Yes/No	$\sigma_{1\,wh-word}$ :: intervenors$_{wh-word}(\sigma_1 ... \tau_1)$
Memory		
DISTANCE	String Position	$\tau_1 - \sigma_1$
DLT	Count	intervenors$_{nom}(\sigma_1 ... \tau_1)$
INTERVENORS	POS	intervenors$_{nom}(\sigma_1 ... \tau_1)$
STACK1NEXT	POS	$\sigma_1 :: \tau_1$
STACK2NEXT	POS	$\sigma_1 :: \sigma_2 :: \tau_1$
STACK3NEXT	POS	$\sigma_1 :: \sigma_2 :: \sigma_3 :: \tau_1$
ACTIVATION	Value	baselineActivation(σ_1)
INTERFERENCE	Value	interference(σ_1)
RETRIEVAL	Time (ms.)	retrievalTime(σ_1)

Table 5: Feature specification. :: indicates concatenation.

recent retrievals at time t_j. This implementation follows standard ACT-R practice in setting the decay rate d to 0.5 (Lewis and Vasishth, 2005; Anderson, 2005).

$$B_i = \ln\left(\sum_{j=1}^{n} t_j^{-d}\right) \tag{2}$$

σ_1's activation can decrease if *competitors*, or other words with similar grammatical categories, have already been parsed. In Equation (1), W_j denotes weights associated with the retrieval cues j that are shared with these competitors, and S_{ji} symbolizes the strengths of association between cues j and the retrieved item i (σ_1). For this model, weights are set to 1 because there is only one retrieval cue j in operation: the POS. The strength of association S_{ji} is computed as in Equation 3.

$$S_{ji} = S_{\max} - \ln(\text{fan}_j) \tag{3}$$

The fan, fan$_j$, is the number of words that have the same grammatical category as cue j, the POS. The maximum degree of association between similar items in memory is $S_{\max}$ which is set to 1.5 following Lewis & Vasishth.

To get the retrieval time, in milliseconds, of σ_1, the activation value calculated in Equation 1 is inserted in Equation 4. The implementation follows Lewis & Vasishth in setting F to 0.14.

$$T_i = Fe^{-A_i} \tag{4}$$

The time T_i is the quantity the parser is sensitive to in determining attachments based on the RETRIEVAL feature. Because it is possible that SUVs are better modeled by only part of the retrieval equation, such as baseline activation or interference, the implementation also considers ACTIVATION and INTERFERENCE features. The features are sensitive to the quantities in the addends in Equation 1, B_i and $\sum_j W_j S_{ji}$ respectively.

4 Results

The results focus on whether the parser chooses a `LeftArc` attachment when it is in the configuration depicted in Figure 3 given the grammatical and memory constraints listed in Table 5. Table 8 depicts the outcome, where **Y** signifies a `LeftArc` attachment is preferred and **N** that it is not.

Only one feature correctly patterns with the experimental evidence: INTERVENORS. It allows a `LeftArc` in the which.which condition, and disallows the arc in other conditions. The INTERVENORS feature also patterns with the experimental evidence as more memory is added. Table 9 depicts the `LeftArc` attachment for increasing levels of k with this feature. At k=1, the parser only chooses the attachment for the which.which condition. At k=2, the parser chooses the attachment for both which.which and which.bare. At k=3, it chooses the attachment for all conditions. This mimics the decreases in difficulty evident in Figure 1, and provides support for reductionist theories: if memory is restricted (k=1), only the easiest attachment is allowed. As memory increases, more attachments are possible.

INTERVENORS is sensitive to the nominal in-

Condition	b.b	b.w	w.b	w.w
Experiment	**N**	**N**	**N**	**Y**
Grammar				
RELMIN=YES	N	N	N	N
RELMIN=NO	N	N	N	N
Memory				
DISTANCE	N	N	N	N
DLT	N	N	N	N
INTERVENORS	**N**	**N**	**N**	**Y**
STACK1NEXT	N	N	N	N
STACK2NEXT	Y	N	Y	N
STACK3NEXT	Y	Y	Y	Y
ACTIVATION	N	N	N	N
INTERFERENCE	Y	N	N	N
RETRIEVAL	Y	N	N	N

Table 8: `LeftArc` attachments for the experimental data.

Condition	b.b	b.w	w.b	w.w
INTERVENORS K=1	N	N	N	Y
INTERVENORS K=2	N	N	Y	Y
INTERVENORS K=3	Y	Y	Y	Y

Table 9: INTERVENORS allows more attachments as k increases.

tervenors between *which* and *read*. RETRIEVAL, INTERFERENCE, and particularly DLT, should also be sensitive to these intervenors. Despite their similarity, none of these features are able to model the attachment behavior in the experimental data.

The STACK3NEXT feature differs from the other features in that it allows the `LeftArc` attachment to occur in any of the conditions. Although this does not match the interpretation of the experimental results followed in this paper, it leaves open the possibility that the feature could model the data according to a different measure of parsing difficulty, such as surprisal (Hale, 2001).

The RELMIN constraint is not able to model the experimental results for gradience.

5 Discussion

The results demonstrate that modeling the experimental data for SUV gradience requires a parser that can vary memory resources as well as be sensitive to the types of the nominal intervenors currently in memory. The gradience is modeled by increasing memory resources, in the form of increases in the beam-width. This demonstrates the usefulness of varying both the types and amounts of memory resources available in a computational model of human sentence processing.

The positive results from the INTERVENORS feature confirms the discourse accessibility hierarchy encoded in the DLT (Gundel et al., 1993; Warren and Gibson, 2002), but only when *wh*-words are included as nominal intervenors. The results also suggest that it is the *type*, and not just the number of intervenors as suggested by the DLT, that is important.

Further, the INTERVENORS feature does not pattern with the DLT hypothesis. DLT assumes that *increasing* the number of nominal intervenors causes sentence processing difficulty (Gibson, 2000; Warren and Gibson, 2002). Here, the number of intervenors is increased, but sentence processing is relatively easier. This effect is explained by the intrinsic difference between the DLT and INTERVENORS features: INTERVENORS provides more information to the parser, in the form of the POS of all intervenors. This indicates that certain intervenors help, rather than hinder, the retrieval process.

The negative results demonstrate that other representations of memory do not model SUV gradience. If we consider this along the continuum from (4), those features that take into account less information than INTERVENORS (DISTANCE and DLT) are too restrictive. Of those features that are more complex than INTERVENORS, many are too permissive, or permit the wrong attachments. This pattern is also visible in the STACKNEXT features: STACK1NEXT is too restrictive, while STACK3NEXT too permissive. STACK2NEXT unfortunately permits the wrong attachments. This pattern in the continuum indicates that an intermediate amount of memory information is required to adequately model these results.

INTERFERENCE, which also considers competitors in the intervening string, would seem likely to pattern with the INTERVENORS results. In fact, similarity-based interference and retrieval have previously been argued to account for these gradience patterns (Hofmeister et al., Submitted). However, the only words considered as competitors with *which* for both features in this model are other *wh*-words. For the which.which condition, for example, INTERFERENCE would only consider the second *which* a competitor. INTERVENORS, on the other hand, considers *book*, *which*, and *student* as possible intervenors. This suggests that the INTERFERENCE measure in retrieval would be more accurate if it considered more competitors, a consideration for future work.

Hofmeister (2007) suggests that it is not a single memory factor, but a number of factors, that contribute to SUV gradience. Some features, such as INTERFERENCE or DLT, may be more accurate when they are considered in addition to other features. It is also likely that probabilistic models that include many features will be more robust than single-feature models, particularly when tested on similar phenomena, like islands. I leave these possibilities to future work.

Although the variable beam-width INTERVENORS feature patterns well with the Arnon et al. results, it does not capture the reading time difference between the bare.bare and the bare.which conditions; both are unavailable at k=2 and available at k=3. Although this may indicate a problem with the feature itself, it is also possible that a more gradient evaluation technique is needed. As suggested in Section 4, determining accuracy on the basis of attachment alone may be insufficient to correctly model the full experimental evidence in terms of reading times. This is an empirical question that can be tested with this computational model. In future work, I consider the role of parser difficulty, via linking hypotheses such as surprisal, in modeling the experimental data.

The interpretation of Relativized Minimality used here as a grammatical constraint could not derive the experimental results. `LeftArc` is not preferred when the parser is in a SUV context (RELMIN=Yes)–an expected result as attachments should not occur in SUV contexts. However, the which.which, which.bare, and the bare.which conditions are not violations because they include non-referential NPs. Even with the RELMIN=NO feature, the parser does not select `LeftArc` attachments, suggesting grammatical gradience is not useful in modeling the SUV gradience results.

This model does not attempt to capture experimental evidence that SUVs and similar phenomena, like islands, are better modeled by grammatical constraints (Phillips, 2006; Sprouse et al., Submitted). Not only does this work only focus on one kind of grammatical constraint for SUV gradience, but the results reported here do not reveal whether the intervention effect itself is better modeled by grammatical or reductionist factors. Rather, the results demonstrate that the *gradience* in the intervention effect is better modeled by memory than by the gradient grammatical feature. Future work with this computational model will allow for an examination of those memory factors and grammatical factors most useful in exploring the source of the intervention effect itself.

6 Conclusion

This study considers grammatical and memory-based explanations for SUV gradience in a human sentence processing model. The results suggest that gradience is best modeled by a parser that can vary memory resources while being sensitive to the types of nominal intervenors that have been parsed. Grammatical and other memory constraints do not determine correct attachments in the SUV environment. The results argue for a theory of language that accounts for SUV gradience in terms of specific memory factors.

Acknowledgments

I am grateful to Sam Epstein, John T. Hale, Philip Hofmeister, Rick Lewis, Colin Phillips, students of the University of Michigan *Rational Behavior and Minimalist Inquiry* course, and two anonymous reviewers for helpful comments and suggestions on this work.

References

S. Abney. 1987. *The English noun phrase in its sentential aspect*. Ph.D. thesis, MIT, Cambridge, MA.

J. R. Anderson. 2005. Human symbol manipulation within an integrated cognitive architecture. *Cognitive Science*, 29:313–341.

I. Arnon, N. Snider, P. Hofmeister, T. F. Jaeger, and I. Sag. To appear. Cross-linguistic variation in a processing account: The case of multiple wh-questions. In *Proceedings of Berkeley Linguistics Society*, volume 32.

M. F. Boston, J. T. Hale, R. Kliegl, and S. Vasishth. 2008. Surprising parser actions and reading difficulty. In *Proceedings of ACL-08: HLT Short Papers*, pages 5–8.

N. Chomsky. 1973. Conditions on transformations. In Stephen Anderson and Paul Kiparsky, editors, *A Festschrift for Morris Halle*, pages 232–286. Holt, Reinhart and Winston, New York.

W. N. Francis and H. Kucera. 1979. Brown corpus manual. Technical report, Department of Linguistics, Brown University, Providence, RI.

E. Gibson. 1998. Linguistic complexity: locality of syntactic dependencies. *Cognition*, 68:1–76.

E. Gibson. 2000. Dependency locality theory: A distance-based theory of linguistic complexity. In A. Marantz, Y. Miyashita, and W. O'Neil, editors, *Image, language, brain: Papers from the First Mind Articulation Symposium*. MIT Press, Cambridge, MA.

P. C. Gordon, R. Hendrick, and W. H. Levine. 2002. Memory-load interference in syntactic processing. *Psychological Science*, 13(5):425–430.

D. J. Grodner and E. A. F. Gibson. 2005. Consequences of the serial nature of linguistic input for sentential complexity. *Cognitive Science*, 29:261–91.

J. K. Gundel, N. Hedberg, and R. Zacharski. 1993. Cognitive status and the form of referring expressions in discourse. *Language*, 69:274–307.

J. T. Hale. 2001. A probabilistic earley parser as a psycholinguistic model. In *Proceedings of NAACL 2001*, pages 1–8.

J. A. Hawkins. 1999. Processing complexity and filler-gap dependencies across grammars. *Language*, 75(2):244–285.

D. G. Hays. 1964. Dependency Theory: A formalism and some observations. *Language*, 40:511–525.

P. Hofmeister, I. Arnon, T. F. Jaeger, I. A. Sag, and N. Snider. Submitted. The source ambiguity problem: distinguishing the effects of grammar and processing on acceptability judgments. *Language and Cognitive Processes*.

P. Hofmeister. 2007. Retrievability and gradience in filler-gap dependencies. In *Proceedings of the 43rd Regional Meeting of the Chicago Linguistics Society*, Chicago. University of Chicago Press.

R. Johansson and P. Nugues. 2007. Extended constituent-to-dependency conversion for English. In *Proceedings of NODALIDA 2007*, Tartu, Estonia.

M. A. Just and P.A. Carpenter. 1992. A capacity theory of comprehension: Individual differences in working memory. *Psychological Review*, 98:122–149.

M. A. Just and S. Varma. 2007. The organization of thinking: What functional brain imaging reveals about the neuroarchitecture of complex cognition. *Cognitive, Affective, and Behavioral Neuroscience*, 7(3):153–191.

L. Karttunen. 1977. Syntax and semantics of questions. *Linguistics and Philosophy*, 1:3–44.

R. Lewis and S. Vasishth. 2005. An activation-based model of sentence processing as skilled memory retrieval. *Cognitive Science*, 29:1–45.

C.-J. Lin, R. C. Weng, and S. S. Keerthi. 2008. Trust region newton method for large-scale regularized logistic regression. *Journal of Machine Learning Research*, 9.

B. McElree. 2000. Sentence comprehension is mediated by content-addressable memory structures. *Journal of Psycholinguistic Research*, 29(2):111–123.

J. Nivre. 2004. Incrementality in deterministic dependency parsing. In *Proceedings of the Workshop on Incremental Parsing (ACL)*, pages 50–57.

D. Pesetsky. 1987. Wh-in-situ: movement and unselective binding. In Eric Reuland and A. ter Meulen, editors, *The representation of (In)Definiteness*, pages 98–129. MIT Press, Cambridge, MA.

C. Phillips. 2006. The real-time status of island phenomena. *Language*, 82:795–823.

C. Phillips. Submitted. Some arguments and nonarguments for reductionist accounts of syntactic phenomena. *Language and Cognitive Processes*.

O. Rambow and A. K. Joshi. 1994. A processing model for free word-order languages. In Charles Clifton, Jr., Lyn Frazier, and Keith Rayner, editors, *Perspectives on sentence processing*, pages 267–301. Erlbaum, Hillsdale, NJ.

L. Rizzi. 1990. *Relativized Minimality*. MIT Press.

J. Sprouse, M. Wagers, and C. Phillips. Submitted. A test of the relation between working memory capacity and syntactic island effects. http://ling.auf.net/lingBuzz/001042.

L. Tesnière. 1959. *Éléments de syntaxe structurale*. Editions Klincksiek.

J. A. Van Dyke and B. McElree. 2006. Retrieval interference in sentence comprehension. *Journal of Memory and Language*, 55:157–166.

E. Wanner and M. Maratsos. 1978. An ATN approach in comprehension. In Morris Halle, Joan Bresnan, and George Miller, editors, *Linguistic theory and psychological reality*, pages 119–161. MIT Press, Cambridge, MA.

T. Warren and Edward Gibson. 2002. The influence of referential processing on sentence complexity. *Cognition*, 85:79–112.

Close = Relevant? The Role of Context in Efficient Language Production

Ting Qian and T. Florian Jaeger
Department of Brain and Cognitive Sciences
University of Rochester
Rochester, NY 14627 United States
{tqian, fjaeger}@bcs.rochester.edu

Abstract

We formally derive a mathematical model for evaluating the effect of context relevance in language production. The model is based on the principle that distant contextual cues tend to gradually lose their relevance for predicting upcoming linguistic signals. We evaluate our model against a hypothesis of efficient communication (Genzel and Charniak's Constant Entropy Rate hypothesis). We show that the development of entropy throughout discourses is described significantly better by a model with cue relevance decay than by previous models that do not consider context effects.

1 Introduction

In this paper, we present a study on the effect of context relevance decay on the entropy of linguistic signals in natural discourses. Context relevance decay refers to the phenomenon that contextual cues that are distant from an upcoming event (e.g. production of a new linguistic signal) are less likely to be relevant to the event, as discourse contents that are close to one another are likely to be semantically related. One can also view the words and sentences in a discourse as time steps, where distant context becomes less relevant simply due to normal forgetting over time (e.g. activation decay in memory). The present study investigates how this decaying property of discourse context might affect the development of entropy of linguistic signals in discourses. We first introduce the background on efficient language production and then propose our hypothesis.

1.1 Background on Efficient Language Production

The metaphor "communication channel", borrowed from Shannon's information theory (Shannon, 1948), can be conceived of as an abstract entity that defines the constraints of language communication (e.g. ambient noise, distortions in articulation). For error free communication to occur, the ensemble of messages that a speaker may utter must be encoded in a system of signals whose entropy is under the capacity of the communication channel. Entropy of these signals, in this context, correlates with the average number of upcoming messages that the speaker can choose from for a particular signal (e.g. a word to be spoken) given preceding discourse context. In other words, if the average number of choices given any linguistic signal exceeds the channel capacity, it cannot be guaranteed that the receiver can correctly infer the originally intended message. Such transmission errors will reduce the efficiency of language communication.

Keeping the entropy of linguistic signals below the channel capacity alone is not efficient, for one can devise a code where each signal corresponds to a distinct message. With a unique choice per signal, this encoding achieves an entropy of zero at the cost of requiring a look-up table that is too large to be possible (cf. Zipf (1935), who makes a similar argument for meaning and form). In fact, the most efficient code requires language users to encode messages into signals of the entropy bounded by the capacity of the channel. One implication of this efficient encoding is that over time, the entropy of the signals is constant. One of the first studies to investigate such constancy is Genzel and Charniak (2002), in which the authors proposed the Constant Entropy Rate (CER) hypothesis: in written text, the entropy per signal symbol is constant across sentence positions in discourses. That is, if we view sentence positions as a measure of time steps, then the entropy per word at each step should be the same in order to achieve efficient communication (word is selected as the unit of signal, although it does not have to

Proceedings of the 2010 Workshop on Cognitive Modeling and Computational Linguistics, ACL 2010, pages 45–53,
Uppsala, Sweden, 15 July 2010.

be case; cf. Qian and Jaeger (2009)).

The difficulty in testing this *direct* prediction is computationally specifying the code used by human speakers to obtain a context-sensitive estimate of the entropy per word. An *n*gram model overestimates the entropy of upcoming messages by relying on only the preceding *n-1* words within a sentence, while in reality the upcoming message is also constrained by extra-sentential context that accumulates within a discourse. The more extra-sentential context that the *n*gram model ignores, the higher estimate for entropy will be. Hence, the CER hypothesis indirectly predicts that the entropy of signals, as estimated by *n*grams, will increase across sentence positions. While some studies have found the predicted positive correlation between sentence position and the per-word entropy of signals estimated by *n*grams, most of them assumed the correlation to be linear (Genzel and Charniak, 2002; Genzel and Charniak, 2003; Keller, 2004; Piantadosi and Gibson, 2008). However, in previous work, we found that a log-linear regression model was a better fit for empirical data than a simple linear regression model based on data of 12 languages (Qian and Jaeger, under review). Why this would be case remained a puzzle.

Our research question is closely related to this *indirect* prediction of the Constant Entropy Rate hypothesis. Intuitively, the number of possible messages that a speaker can choose from for an upcoming signal in a discourse is often restricted by the presence of discourse context. Contextual cues in the preceding discourse can make the upcoming content more predictable and thus effectively reduces signal entropy. As previously mentioned, however, different contextual cues, depending on how long ago they were provided, have various degrees of effectiveness in reducing signal entropy. Thus we ask the question whether the decay of context relevance could explain the sublinear relation between entropy and discourse progress that has been observed in previous studies.

We formally derive two nonlinear models for testing our Relevance Decay Hypothesis (introduced next). In addition to the constant entropy assumption in CER, our model assumed that the relevance of early sentences in the discourse systematically decays as a function of discourse progress. Our models provide the best fit to the distribution of entropy of signals, suggesting the availability of discourse context can affect the planning of the rest of a discourse.

1.2 Relevance Decay Hypothesis

We hypothesize the sublinear relation between the entropy of signals, when estimated out of discourse context (hereafter, *out-of-context* entropy of signals) using an *n*gram model, and sentence position (Piantadosi and Gibson, 2008; Qian and Jaeger, under review) is due to the role of discourse context (hereafter, *context*). Consider the following example. Assume that context at the kth sentence position comes from the $1 \ldots k-1$ sentences in the past. If k is large enough, context from the early sentences $1 \ldots i$ ($i \ll k$) is essentially no longer relevant. Rather, the nearby $k-i$ sentences are contributing most of the discourse context. As a result, the constraint on the entropy of signals at sentence position k is *mostly* due to the nearby window of $k-i$ sentences. Then if we look ahead to the $(k+1)$th sentence position and follow the same steps of reasoning, context at that point also mostly comes from the nearby window of $k-i$ sentences (i.e. $(k+1)-(i+1)=k-i$). Hence, for later sentence positions, the difference in available context is minimal. Consequently, their out-of-context entropy of signals increases at a very small rate. On the other hand, when k is fairly small, to the extent that the $k-i$ window covers the entire preceding discourse, all of the $1 \ldots k-1$ sentences are contributing relevant context. As k increases, the number of preceding sentences increases, which results in a more significant change in relevant context, but the relevance of each individual sentence decreases with its distance to k, which results in a sublinear pattern of relevant context with respect to sentence position overall. As we will show, the relation of out-of-context entropy of signals to sentence position follows from the relation of relevant context to sentence position, exhibiting a sublinear form as well.

The problem of interest here is to specify how quickly the relevance of a preceding sentence decays as a function of its distance to a target sentence position k. We experimented with two forms of decay functions – power law decay and exponential decay. It has been established that many types of human behaviors can be well described by the power function (Wixted and Ebbesen, 1991), so we mainly focus on building a model under the

Language	Training Data		Test Data		
	in words	*in sentences*	*in words*	*in sentences*	*per position*
Danish	154,514	5,640	8,048	270	18
Dutch	50,309	3,255	2,105	90	6
English	597,698	23,295	31,276	1155	77
French	229,461	9,300	11,371	435	29
Italian	97,198	4,245	4,524	225	15
Mandarin Chinese	145,127	4,875	4,310	150	10
Norwegian	89,724	4,125	2,973	150	10
Portuguese	170,342	5,340	9,044	240	16
Russian	398,786	18,075	20,668	930	62
Spanish (Latin-American)	1,363,560	41,160	67,870	2,070	138
Spanish (European)	255,366	7,485	8,653	240	16
Swedish	266,348	11,535	13,369	555	37

Table 1: Number of words and sentences in the training and test data for each of the twelve languages. The last column gives the number of sentences at each sentence position (which is identical to the number of documents contained in the corpora).

power law, and examine if the model under the exponential law yields any difference. Under the assumptions of true entropy rate is constant across sentences, we predict that our models will better characterize the changes in estimated entropy of signals than general regression models that are blind to the role of context.

2 Methods

2.1 Data

We used the Reuters Corpus Volume 1 and 2 (Lewis et al., 2004). The corpus contains about 810,000 English news articles and over 487,000 news articles in thirteen languages. Because of inconsistent annotation, we excluded the data from three languages, Chinese, German, and Japanese. For Chinese, we substituted the Treebank Corpus (Xue et al., 2005) for the Reuters data, leaving us with twelve languages: Danish, Dutch, English, French, Italian, Mandarin Chinese, Norwegian, Portuguese, Russian, European Spanish, Latin-American Spanish, and Swedish. In order to estimate out-of-context entropy per word (i.e. per signal symbol) for each sentence position, articles were divided into a training set (95% of all stories) for training language models and a test set (the remaining 5%) for analysis (see Table 1 for details). Out-of-context entropy per word was estimated by computing the average log probability of sentences at that position, normalized by their lengths in words (i.e. for an individual sentence token s, the term to be averaged is $\frac{-\log p(s)}{length(s)}$ *bits* per word). Standard trigram language models were used to compute these probabilities (Clarkson and Rosenfeld, 1997). The majority of the 12 languages belong to the Indo-European family, while Mandarin Chinese is a Sino-Tibetan language.

2.2 Modeling Relevance Decay of Context

Formally, we define the relevance of context in the same unit as entropy of signals – bits per word. Let r_0 denote the entropy of signals that efficiently encode the ensemble of messages a speaker can choose from for any sentence position, a constant under the assumption of CER. According to Information Theory, r_0 is equivalent to the uncertainty associated with any sentence position if context is considered. Thus, in error free communication, linguistic signals presented at the kth sentence position are said to have resolved the uncertainty at k and therefore are r_0-bit relevant at the kth sentence position. Then, at the $(k+i)$th sentence position, these linguistic signals have become context by definition and their relevance has decayed to some r bits. Our models start from defining the value of r as a function of the distance between context and a target sentence position.

2.2.1 Power-law Decay Model

If the relevance of a cue q (e.g. a preceding sentence), which is originally r_0-bit relevant at position k_q, decays at the rate following the power function, its remaining relevance at target sentence position k is:

$$relevance_{pow}(k, q) = r_0(k - k_q + 1)^{-\lambda} \quad (1)$$

In Equation (1), $k > k_q$ and λ is the decay rate. This means at position k, the relevance of the cue from the $(k-1)$th sentence is $r_0 * 2^{-\lambda}$-bit relevant; the relevance of the cue from the $(k-2)$th sentence is $r_0 * 3^{-\lambda}$-bit relevant, and so on. As a result, the relevance of discourse-specific context at position k is the marginalization of all cues up to q_{k-1}:

$$context_{pow}(k) = r_0 \sum_{q_i \in \{q_1 \cdots q_{k-1}\}} (k - k_{q_i} + 1)^{-\lambda} \quad (2)$$

The general trend predicted by Equation (2) is that discourse-specific context increases more rapidly at the beginning of a discourse and much more slowly towards the end due to the relevance decay of distant cues. Rewriting Equation (2) in a closed-form formula so that a model can be fitted to data is not a trivial task without knowing the rate λ, but the paradox is that λ has to be estimated from the data. As a workaround, we approximated the value of Equation (2) by computing a definite integral of Equation (1), where Δi is a shorthand for $k - k_q + 1$:

$$\begin{aligned} context_{pow}(k) &\approx \int_1^k r_0 \Delta i^{-\lambda} d\Delta i \\ &= r_0 (\frac{k^{1-\lambda} - 1}{1 - \lambda}) \end{aligned} \quad (3)$$

Equation (3) uses an integral to approximate the sum of a series defined as a function. The result is usually acceptable as long as λ is greater than 1 so that the series defined by Equation 1 is convergent (this assumption is empirically supported; see Figure 5). Note that Equation (3) produces the desirable effect that upon encountering the first sentence of a discourse, no discourse-specific contextual cues are available to the speaker (i.e. $context(1) = 0$).

Now that we know the maximum relevance of context at sentence position k, we can predict the amount of out-of-context entropy of signals $r(k)$ based on the idea of uncertainty again. There are new linguistic signals that are r_0-bit relevant *in context* at any sentence position. In addition, we now know $context(k)$ bits of relevant context are also available. Thus, the sum of r_0 and $context(k)$ defines the maximum amount of out-of-context uncertainty that can be resolved at sentence position k. Therefore, the out-of-context entropy of signals at k is at most:

$$\begin{aligned} r_{pow}(k) &= context(k) + r_0 \\ &= r_0 \frac{k^{1-\lambda} - 1}{1 - \lambda} + r_0 \end{aligned} \quad (4)$$

Whether speakers will utilize all available context as predicted by Equation (4) is another debate. Here we adopt the view that speakers are maximally efficient in that they do make use of all available context. Thus, we make the prediction that out-of-context entropy of signals, as observed empirically from data, can be described by this model. Figure 1 shows the behavior of this function with various parameter sets.

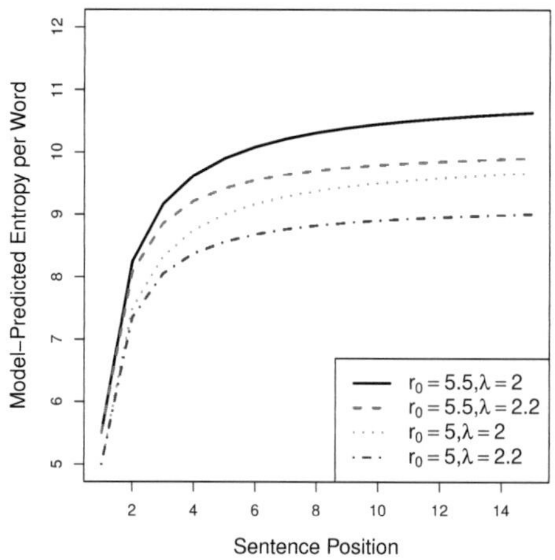

Figure 1: Schematic plots of the behavior of out-of-context entropy of signals assuming the decay of the relevance of context is a power function.

2.2.2 Exponential Decay Model

The second model assumes the relevance of context decays exponentially. Following the same notations as before, the relevance of a cue q at position k is:

$$relevance_{exp}(k, q) = r_0 e^{-\lambda(k - k_q)} \quad (5)$$

The major difference between the power function and the exponential one is that the relevance of a contextual cue drops more slowly in the exponential case (Anderson, 1995). The relevance of all discourse-specific context for a speaker at k is:

$$context_{exp}(k) = r_0 \sum_{i=1}^{k-1} e^{-\lambda i} \quad (6)$$

Equation (6) is the sum of a geometric progression series. We can write Equation (6) in a closed-form:

$$context_{exp}(k) = \frac{r_0}{e^{\lambda} - 1}(1 - e^{-(k-1)\lambda}) \quad (7)$$

As a result, the out-of-context entropy of signals is:

$$r_{exp}(k) = \frac{r_0}{e^{\lambda} - 1}(1 - e^{-(k-1)\lambda}) + r_0 \quad (8)$$

Figure 2 schematically shows the behavior of this function. One can notice this function converges against a ceiling more quickly than the power function. Thus, this model makes a slightly different prediction from the power law model.

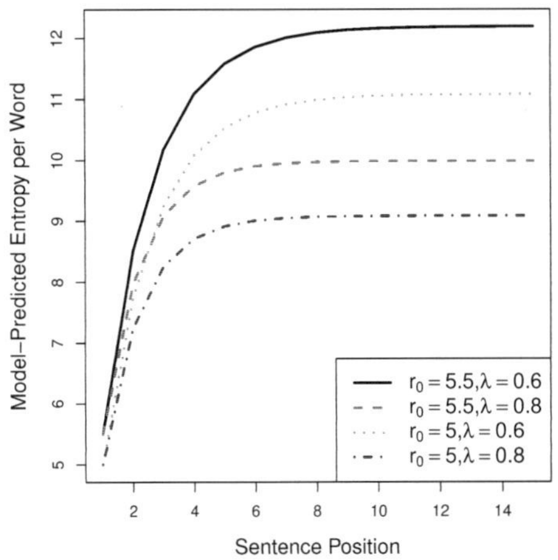

Figure 2: Schematic plots of the behavior of out-of-context entropy of signals assuming the decay of the relevance of context is an exponential function.

2.3 Nonlinear Regression Analysis

To test whether the proposed models (i.e. Equations 4 and 8) better characterize the data, we built nonlinear regression models with document-specific random effects, where the out-of-context entropy of signals, r_{ij}, is regressed on sentence position, k_j. Based on the power law model, we have

$$r_{ij} = (\beta_1 + b_{1i})\frac{{k_j}^{1-\beta_2} - 1}{1 - \beta_2} + (\beta_1 + b_{1i}) + \epsilon_{ij} \quad (9)$$

where β_1 corresponds to r_0, the theoretical constant entropy of signals under an ideal encoding. b_{1i} represents the document-specific deviations from the overall mean. β_2 corresponds to λ, the mean rate at which the relevance of a past cue decays, which is unfortunately not considered for random effects for the practical purpose of making computation feasible in the current work. Finally, ϵ_{ij} represents the errors independently distributed as $\mathcal{N}(0, \sigma^2)$, orthogonal to document specific deviations.

For the exponential model, the nonlinear model is the following (symbols have the same interpretations as in Equation 9):

$$r_{ij} = \frac{(\beta_1 + b_{1i})}{e^{\beta_2} - 1}(1 - e^{-(k_j-1)\beta_2}) + (\beta_1 + b_{1i}) + \epsilon_{ij} \quad (10)$$

Fitting data with the above nonlinear models requires starting estimates for fixed-effect coefficients (i.e. β_1s and β_2s). Unfortunately, there are no principled methods for selecting these values. We heuristically selected 6 for β_1 and 2 for β_2 as starting values for the power law model, and 4 and 0.5 as starting values for the exponential model.

3 Results

We examined the quality of the models and the parameters in the models: r_0, the within-context entropy rate, and λ, the rate of context decay.

3.1 Model Quality Comparison

The CER hypothesis indirectly predicts that out-of-context entropy of signals of sentence positions (bits per word) should increase throughout a discourse. The two models go one step further to predict specific sublinear increase patterns, based on the speaker's considerations of the relevance of past contextual cues. We compared the quality of models in terms of Bayesian Information Criterion (BIC) *within languages*. A lower BIC score indicates a better fit. As shown by Figure 3, we find our models best explain the data in 9 out of the 12 languages, reporting lower BIC scores than both the linear and log-linear models as reported in our previous work (Qian and Jaeger, under review). For Danish, English and Italian, although neither of our models produced a better score than the log-linear model, the relative difference is small: 0.54 on average (comparing to BIC scores on the order of 10^2 to 10^3).

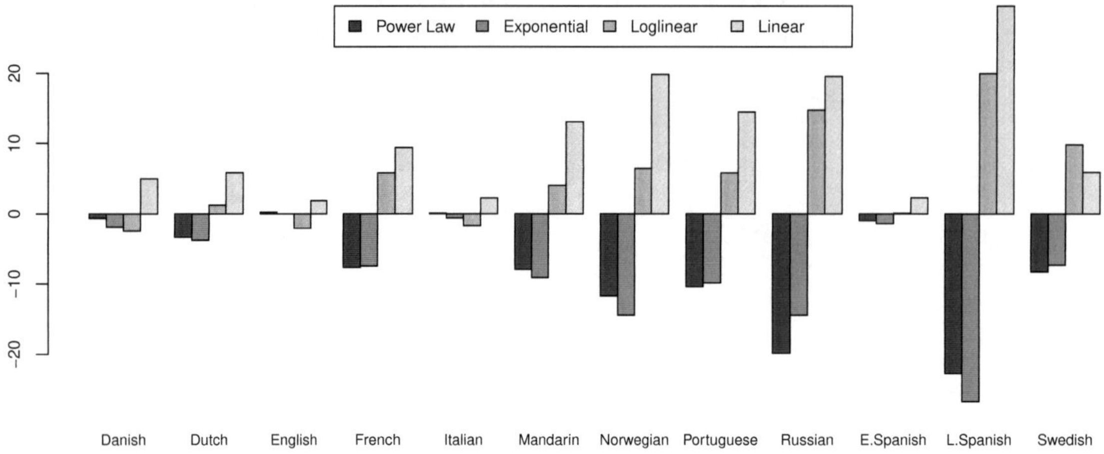

Figure 3: Our models yield superior BIC scores in most languages. The y-axis shows the differences between BIC scores of individual models for a language and mean BIC of the models for that language (*E.Spanish* = European Spanish; *L.Spanish* = Latin-American Spanish).

Specifically, in terms of BIC scores, the power-law model is better than the linear model ($t(11) = -3.98$, $p < 0.01$), and the log-linear model ($t(11) = -3.10$, $p < 0.05$). The exponential model is also better than the linear model ($t(11) = -3.98$, $p < 0.01$), and the log-linear model ($t(11) = -3.18$, $p < 0.01$). The power-law model and the exponential model are not significantly different from each other ($t(11) = 0.5$, $p > 0.5$).

3.2 Interpretation of Parameters

Constant Entropy of Signals r_0. Both models are constructed in such a way that the first parameter r_0, in theory, corresponds to the theoretical within-context entropy of signals of sentence positions. This parameter refers to how many bits per word are needed to encode the ensemble of messages at a sentence position when context is taken into account. The CER hypothesis directly predicts that this rate should be constant throughout a discourse. Although we are unable to test this prediction directly, it is nevertheless interesting to compare whether these two independently developed models yield the same estimates for this parameter in each language.

Figure 4 shows encouraging results. Not only the estimates made by the power model are well correlated with those by the exponential model, but also the slope of this correlation is equal to 1 ($t(10) = 1.01$, $p < 0.0001$). Since there are no reasons *a priori* to suspect that these two models

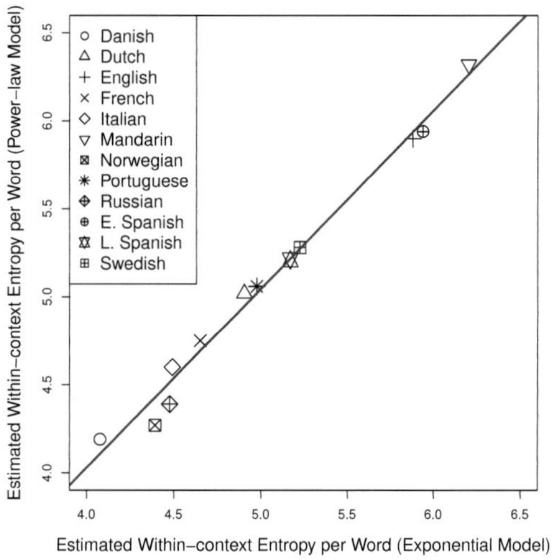

Figure 4: Estimates of r_0 correlate between both models with a slope of 1.

would give the same estimates, this is a first step to confirming the entropy per word in sentence production is indeed a tractable constant throughout discourses.

Among all languages, r_0 has a mean of 5.0 bits in both models, and a variance of 0.46 in the power-law model and 0.48 in the exponential model, both remarkably small. The similarity in r_0 between languages may lead one to speculate whether the amount of uncertainty per word in discourses is largely the same regardless of the actual language used by the speakers. On the other hand, the differences in r_0 may reveal the specific properties of different languages. Meanwhile, precautions need to be taken in interpreting those estimates given that the corpora are of different sizes, and the *n*gram model is simplistic in nature.

Decay Rate λ. The second parameter λ corresponds to the rate of relevance decay in both models. Since the base relevance r_0 varies between languages, λ can be more intuitively interpreted as to indicate the percentage of the original relevance of a contextual cue still remains in n positions. In the power-law model, for example, the context information from a previous sentence in Danish, on average, is only 11.6% ($2^{-3.10} = 0.116$) as relevant. Hence, the relevance of a contextual cue decreases rather quickly for Danish. Table 2 shows this is in fact the general picture for all languages we tested.

Language	**Relevance of Context in Discourse** (%)		
	1 pos. before	*2 pos. before*	*3 pos. before*
Danish	11.6	3.3	1.4
Dutch	10.4	2.8	1.1
English	0.1	0.0	0.0
French	8.5	2.0	0.7
Italian	10.2	2.7	1.0
Mandarin	7.7	1.7	0.6
Norwegian	18.9	7.1	3.6
Portuguese	5.5	1.0	0.3
Russian	12.7	3.8	1.6
E. Spanish	0.8	0.0	0.0
L. Spanish	2.7	0.3	0.1
Swedish	5.8	1.1	0.3

Table 2: In the power model, relevance of a contextual cue decays rather quickly for each language.

The picture of λ looks a little different in the exponential model. The relevance percentage on average is significantly higher, which confirms an earlier point that the power function decreases more quickly than the exponential function. Table 3 shows a summary for the 12 languages.

One may note that the decay rate varies greatly between languages under the prediction of both models. However, these number are only approximations since the entropy estimated by the *n*gram language model is far from psychological reality. Furthermore, it is unlikely that speakers of one language would exhibit the same decay rate of context relevance in their production, let alone speakers of different languages, who may be subject to language-specific constraints during production. Therefore, the variation in estimates of λ seems reasonable.

Language	**Relevance of Context in Discourse** (%)		
	1 pos. before	*2 pos. before*	*3 pos. before*
Danish	30.1	9.1	2.7
Dutch	28.7	8.2	2.4
English	9.6	0.9	0.1
French	26.7	7.1	1.9
Italian	28.7	8.2	2.4
Mandarin	25.7	6.6	1.7
Norwegian	42.3	17.9	7.6
Portuguese	22.5	5.1	1.1
Russian	34.6	12.0	4.2
E. Spanish	14.2	2.0	0.3
L. Spanish	18.6	3.5	0.6
Swedish	23.7	5.6	1.3

Table 3: In the exponential model, relevance of a contextual cue decays more slowly.

Correlation between r_0 and λ. Interestingly, r_0 and λ are highly correlated ($r^2 = 0.39, p < 0.05$ in the power model, Figure 5; $r^2 = 0.47, p < 0.01$ in the exponential model, Figure 6): a high relevance decay rate tends to be coupled with high within-context entropy of signals. This unanticipated observation is in fact compatible with the account of efficient language production: a high within-context entropy of signals indicates the base relevance of a contextual cue (i.e. r_0) is high. It is then useful for its relevance to decay more quickly to allow the speaker to integrate context from other cues. Otherwise, the total amount of relevant context may presumably overload working memory. However, our current results come from only cross-linguistic samples. Cross-validation in within-language samples is needed for confirming this hypothesis.

3.3 The Bigger Picture

Having obtained the estimates for r_0 and λ, we are now in a position to examine how out-of-context entropy of signals increases as a function of sentence positions, given the estimates of these two parameters. As shown in Figure 7, the predictions from both models are qualitative similar except that 1) when the decay rate in the power-law model is low, out-of-context entropy of signals converges more slowly than in the exponential model (Figure 7, right panel); 2) when the decay rate in the power model is high, it almost converges as quickly as the exponential model, and only minor differences exist in their predictions (Figure 7, left panel).

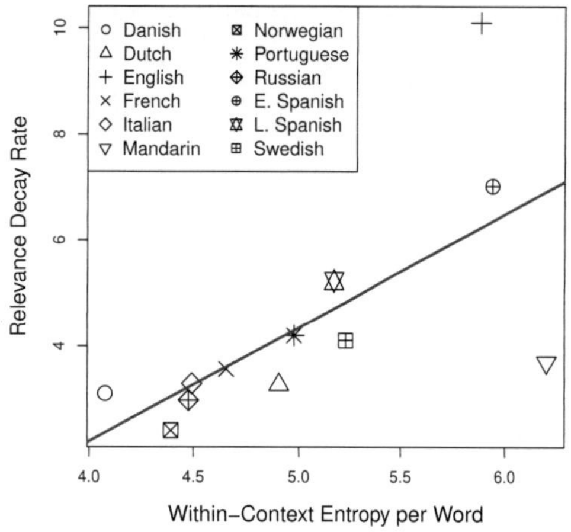

Figure 5: The rate of relevance decay is correlated with within-context entropy of signals in the power-law model.

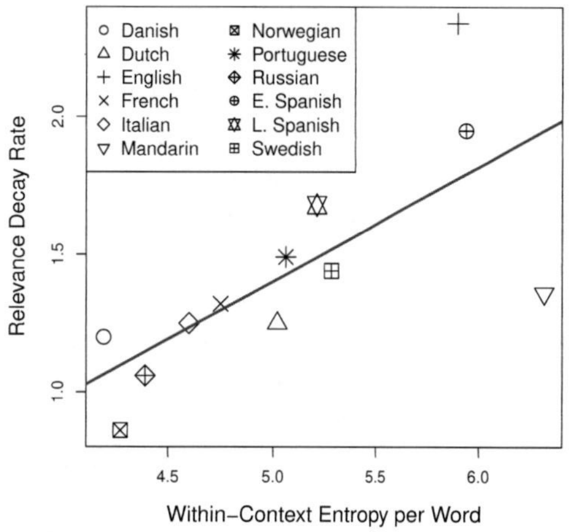

Figure 6: The rate of relevance decay is correlated with within-context entropy of signals in the exponential model.

Because of the nonlinearity in our models, it is not possible to report the results in an intuitive manner as in "an increase in sentence position corresponds to an increase of X bits of out-of-context entropy per word". Instead, we can analytically solve for the derivative of the predicted out-of-context entropy of signals with respect to sentence position (Equation 4 and 8). This gives us:

$$r_{power}(k)' = r_0 k^{-\lambda} \tag{11}$$

for the power-law model, showing the rate of increase in predicted out-of-context entropy of signals is a monotonically decreasing power function, and

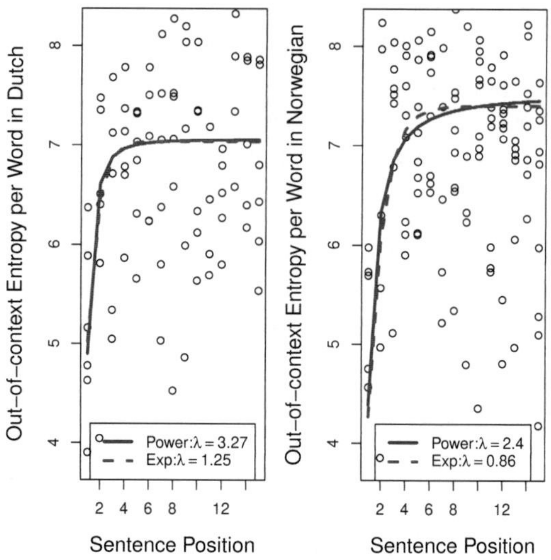

Figure 7: Predicted out-of-context entropy of signals by the power-law model (solid) and the exponential model (dashed) in Dutch and Norwegian, with the actual distributions plotted on the background.

$$r_{exp}(k)' = \frac{r_0 \lambda}{e^{\lambda} - 1}(e^{-(k-1)\lambda}) \tag{12}$$

for the exponential model, showing the rate of increase is a monotonically decreasing exponential function. These mathematical properties indeed match our observations in Figure 7.

4 Discussion and Future Work

The models introduced in this paper try to answer this question: if the relevance of a contextual cue for predicting an upcoming linguistic signal decays over the course of a discourse, how much uncertainty (entropy) is associated with each individual sentence position? We have shown under that models that incorporate (power law or exponential) cue relevance decay in most cases describe the relation of out-of-context entropy of signals to sentence position are better accounted for than previously suggested models.

We are continuing to investigate along this line. Specifically, we are interested in finding the role of semantic memory in affecting the relevance decay of context. To test that, we plan to implement a probabilistic topic model, in which topic continuity between a preceding sentence and an upcoming sentence is quantitatively measured. Thus, the decay of contextual cues can be based on the estimated semantic relatedness between sentences, in addition to the abstract notion of *rate* as used in this paper.

Finally, our relevance decay model can be applied to the domain of language processing as well. For instance, the distance between a contextual cue and the target word may affect how quickly a comprehender can process the information conveyed by the word. We plan to address these question in future work.

5 Conclusion

We have presented a new approach for examining the distribution of entropy of linguistic signals in discourses, showing that not only the out-of-context entropy of signals increases sublinearly with sentence position, but also the sublinear trend is better explained by our nonlinear models than by log-linear models of previous work. Our models are built on the assumption that the relevance of a contextual cue for predicting a linguistic signal in the future decays with its distance to the target, and predict the relation of out-of-context entropy of signals to sentence position in discourses. These results indirectly lend support to the hypothesis that speakers maintain a constant entropy of signals across sentence positions in a discourse.

Acknowledgements

We wish to thank Meredith Brown, Alex Fine and three anonymous reviewers for their helpful comments on this paper. This work was supported by NSF grant BCS-0845059 to TFJ.

References

John R. Anderson. 1995. *Learning and Memory: An integrated approach.* John Wiley & Sons.

Philip R. Clarkson and Roni Rosenfeld. 1997. Statistical language modeling using the cmu-cambridge toolkit. In *Proceedings of ESCA Eurospeech.*

Dimitry Genzel and Eugene Charniak. 2002. Entropy rate constancy in text. In *ACL*, pages 199–206.

Dimitry Genzel and Eugene Charniak. 2003. Variation of entropy and parse trees of sentences as a function of the sentence number. in. In *EMNLP*, pages 65–72.

Frank Keller. 2004. The entropy rate principle as a predictor of processing effort: An evaluation against eye-tracking data. In *EMNLP*, pages 317–324.

D. D. Lewis, Y. Yang, T. Rose, and F Li. 2004. Rcv1: A new benchmark collection for text categorization research. *J Mach Learn Res*, 5:361–397.

Steve Piantadosi and Edwards Gibson. 2008. Uniform information density in discourse: a cross-corpus analysis of syntactic and lexical predictability. In *CUNY.*

Ting Qian and T. Florian Jaeger. 2009. Evidence for efficient language production in chinese. In *CogSci09*, pages 851–856.

Ting Qian and T. Florian Jaeger. under review. Entropy profiles in language: A cross-linguistic investigation.

C. E. Shannon. 1948. A mathematical theory of communications. *Bell Labs Tech J*, 27(4):623–656.

J. T. Wixted and E. B. Ebbesen. 1991. On the form of forgetting. *Psychological Science*, 2:409–415.

Nianwen Xue, Fei Xia, Fu-Dong Chiou, and Martha Palmer. 2005. The Penn Chinese TreeBank: Phrase structure annotation of a large corpus. *Nat Lang Eng*, 11:207–238.

G. K. Zipf. 1935. *Psycho-Biology of Languages.* Houghton-Mifflin.

Predicting Cognitively Salient Modifiers of the Constitutive Parts of Concepts

Gerhard Kremer and **Marco Baroni**
CIMeC, University of Trento, Italy
(gerhard.kremer|marco.baroni)@unitn.it

Abstract

When subjects describe concepts in terms of their characteristic properties, they often produce *composite* properties, e. g., rabbits are said to have *long* ears, not just ears. We present a set of simple methods to extract the modifiers of composite properties (in particular: parts) from corpora. We achieve our best performance by combining evidence about the association between the modifier and the part both within the context of the target concept and independently of it. We show that this performance is relatively stable across languages (Italian and German) and for production vs. perception of properties.

1 Introduction

Subject-generated concept descriptions in terms of properties of different kinds (category: *rabbits* are *mammals*, parts: they have *long ears*, behaviour: they *jump*, ...) are widely used in cognitive science as proxies to feature-based representations of concepts in the mind (Garrard et al., 2001; McRae et al., 2005; Vinson and Vigliocco, 2008). These *feature norms* (as collections of subject-elicited properties are called in the relevant literature) are used in simulations of cognitive tasks and experimental design. Moreover, vector spaces that have subject-generated properties as dimensions have been shown to be a good complement or alternative to traditional semantic models based on corpus collocates (Andrews et al., 2009; Baroni et al., 2010).

Since the concept–property pairs in feature norms resemble the tuples that relation extraction algorithms extract from corpora (Hearst, 1992; Pantel and Pennacchiotti, 2006), recent research has attempted to extract feature-norm-like concept descriptions from corpora (Almuhareb, 2006; Baroni et al., 2010; Shaoul and Westbury, 2008). From a practical point of view, the success of this enterprise would mean being able to produce much larger norms without the need to resort to expensive and time-consuming elicitation experiments, leading to wider cognitive simulations and possibly better vector space models of semantics. From a theoretical point of view, a corpus-based system that produces human-like concept descriptions might provide cues of how humans themselves come up with such descriptions.

However, the corpus-based models proposed for this task up to this point overlook the fact that subjects very often produce *composite* properties: Subjects state that rabbits have *long* ears, not just ears; cars have *four* wheels; a calf is a *baby* cow, etc. Composite properties are not multi-word expressions in the usual sense. There is nothing special or idiomatic about *long ears*. It is just that we find it to be a remarkable fact about rabbits, worth stating in their description, that their ears are long. In the norms described in section 3, around one third of the part descriptions are composite. Note that while our focus is on feature norms, a similar point about the importance of composite properties could be made for other knowledge repositories of importance to computational linguistics, such as WordNet (Fellbaum, 1998) and ConceptNet (Liu and Singh, 2004), approximately 68,000 (36%) of the entries and 1,300 (32%) of the part entries being composites, respectively.

In this paper, we tackle the problem of generating composite properties from corpus data by simplifying it in various ways. First, we focus on *part* properties only, because they are commonly encountered in feature norms, and because they are are commonly composite (cf. section 3). Second, we assume that an early step in the process of property extraction has already generated a list of simple parts, perhaps using an existing whole–part relation extraction algorithm (Girju et al., 2006). Finally, we focus on composite parts

Proceedings of the 2010 Workshop on Cognitive Modeling and Computational Linguistics, ACL 2010, pages 54–62,
Uppsala, Sweden, 15 July 2010.

with an *adjective–noun* structure – together with *numeral–noun* cases, these constitute the near totality of composite parts in the norms described in section 3. Having thus delimited the scope of our exploration, we will adopt the following terminology: *concept* for the target nominal concept (*rabbit*), *part* for the (nominal) part property (*ear*) and *modifier* for the adjective that makes the part composite (*long*).

We present simple methods that, given a list of concept–part pairs and a POS-tagged and lemmatised corpus, rank and extract candidate modifiers for the parts when predicated of the concepts. We exploit the co-occurrence patterns of the part with the modifier both near the concept and in other contexts (both kinds of co-occurrences turn out to be helpful). We first test our methods on German feature norms, and then we show that they generalise well by applying them to similar data in Italian, and to the same set of German concept–part pairs when evaluated by asking new subjects to rate the top ranked modifiers generated by the ranking methods. This also leads to a more general discussion of differences between modifiers produced by subjects in the elicitation experiment and those that are rated acceptable in perception, and the significance of this for corpus-based property generation.

The paper is structured as follows. After shortly reviewing some related work in section 2, in section 3, we describe our feature norms focusing in particular on composite properties. In section 4, we describe our methods to harvest modifiers from a corpus and report the extraction experiments, whereas section 5 concludes by discussing directions for further work.

2 Related Work

We are not aware of other attempts to extract concept-dependent modifiers of properties. We review instead related work in feature norm collection and prediction, and mention some relevant literature on the extraction of significant co-occurrences from corpora.

Feature-based concept description norms have been collected in psychology for decades. Among the more recent publicly available norms of this sort, there are those collected by Garrard et al. (2001), Vinson and Vigliocco (2008) and McRae et al. (2005). The latter was the main methodological inspiration for the bilingual norms we rely on (see section 3 below). The norms of McRae and colleagues include descriptions of 541 concrete concepts corresponding to English nouns. The 725 subjects that rated these concepts had to list their features on a paper questionnaire. The produced features were then normalised and classified into categories such as *part* and *function* by the experimenters. The published norms include, among other kinds of information, the frequency of production of each feature for a concept by the subjects.

Almuhareb (2006) was the first to attempt to reproduce subject-generated features with text mining techniques. He computed precision and recall measures of various pattern-based feature extraction methods using Vinson and Vigliocco's norms for 35 concepts as a gold standard. The best precision was around 16% at about 11% recall; maximum recall was around 60% with less than 2% precision, confirming how difficult the task is. Importantly for our purposes, Almuhareb removed the modifier from composite features before running the experiments (*1 wheel* converted to *wheel*), thus eschewing the main characteristic of subject-generated concept descriptions that we tackle here. Shaoul and Westbury (2008) and Baroni et al. (2010) used corpus-based semantic space models to predict the top 10 features of 44 concepts from the McRae norms. The best model (Baroni et al.'s Strudel) guesses on average 24% of the human-produced features, again confirming the difficulty of the task. And, again, the test set was pre-processed to remove modifiers of composite features, thus sidestepping the problem we want to deal with. It is worth remarking that, by removing modifiers, previous authors are making the task easier in terms of feature extraction procedure (because the algorithms only need to look for single words), but they also create artificial "salient" features that, once the modifier has been stripped of, are not that salient anymore (what distinguishes a monocycle from a tricycle is that one has 1 wheel, the other 3, not simply having wheels). It is conceivable that a method to assign sensible modifiers to features might actually improve the overall quality of feature extraction algorithms.

Following a very long tradition in computational linguistics (Church and Hanks, 1990), we use co-occurrence statistics for words in certain contexts to hypothesise a meaningful connection between the words. In this respect, what we propose is not different from common methods to extract and rank collocations, multi-word expressions or semantically related terms (Evert, 2008). From a technical point of view, the innovative aspect of our task is that we do not just look for co-occurrences between two items, but for co-occurrences in the context of a third element, i. e., we are interested in modifier–part pairs that are related when predicated of a certain concept. The method we apply to the extraction of modifier–part pairs when they co-occur with the target concept in a large window is similar to the idea of looking for partially untethered contextual patterns proposed by Garera and Yarowsky (2009), that extract name–pattern–property tuples where the pattern and the property must be adjacent, but the target name is only required to occur in the same sentence.

3 Composite Parts in Feature Norms

Our empirical starting point are the feature norms collected in parallel from 73 German and 69 Italian subjects by Kremer et al. (2008), following a methodology similar to that of McRae et al. (2005). The norms pertain to 50 concrete concepts from 10 classes such as mammals (e. g., *dog*), manipulable tools (e. g., *comb*), etc. The concept–part pairs in these norms served on the one hand as input to our algorithm – on the other hand, its output (the set of selected modifiers from the corpus) could be evaluated against those modifiers that were produced by the subjects. Furthermore, the bilingual nature of the norms allows us to tune our algorithm on one language (German), and evaluate its performance on the other (Italian), to assess its cross-lingual generalisation capability.

To confirm that speakers actually frequently produce properties composed of part and modifier, observe that in the German data (10,010 descriptive phrases in total), of the 1,667 parts produced, 625 (more than one third) were composite parts, and 404 were composed of an adjective and a noun, the target of this research work. Looking at the distinct parts that were elicited, 92 were always produced with a modifier, 280 only without modifier, and 122 both with and without modifier. That is, for about 43% of the parts at least some speakers used a composite expression of adjective and noun. This high proportion motivates our work and is not surprising, given that, for describing a specific concept, one will tend to come up with whatever makes this concept special and distinguishes it from other concepts – which (considering parts) sometimes is the part itself (*elephant: trunk*) and sometimes something special about the shape, colour, size, or other attributes of the part (*elephant: big ears*).

The data set for modifier extraction and subsequent method evaluation comprises all the concept–modifier–part triples (e. g., *onion: brown peel*) produced by at least one subject, taken from the German and the Italian norms. The German (Italian) speakers described 41 (30) different concepts by using at least one out of 80 (45) different parts in combination with one out of 62 (50) different modifiers, totalling to 229 (127) differently combined triples.

4 Experiments

This section describes the approach we explored for ranking and extracting modifiers of composite parts and evaluates the performance of 6 different extraction methods in terms of the production norms. Acceptance rate data from a follow-up judgement experiment complete the evaluation.

4.1 Ranked Modifier Lists

Based on the idea that the co-occurrence of words in a text corpus reflects to some extent how strong these words are associated in speakers' minds (Spence and Owens, 1990), our extraction approach works on the lemmatised and POS-tagged German WaCky[1] web corpus of about 1.2 billion tokens.

Modifier–Part Frequencies

Using the CQP[2] tool, corpus frequencies were collected for all co-occurrences of adjectives with those part nouns that were produced in the experiment described above. A possible gap of up to 3 tokens between the pair of adjective and noun allowed to extract also adjectives that are not directly adjacent to the nouns in the corpus (but in a sequence of adjectives, for example). For each part noun, the 5 most frequent adjective modifiers from the ranked modifier–part list were selected under the assumption that the preferred usage of these modifiers with the specific part indicates the most common attributes which that part typically has.

[1]See the WaCky project at `http://wacky.sslmit.unibo.it`

[2]Corpus Query Processor (part of the IMS Open Corpus Workbench, see `http://cwb.sourceforge.net`)

Log-Likelihood Values of Frequencies

An attempt to improve the performance of the first method is to calculate[3] the log-likelihood association value for each modifier–part pair instead of keeping the raw co-occurrence frequency, and select the 5 highest ranked modifiers for each part from this list. Log-likelihood weighting should account for typical modifiers which have a low frequency but do generally not occur often in the corpus, and with not many other parts – their log-likelihood value will be higher, and so will be their rank (e. g., *two-sided blade* in contrast to *long blade*).

Modifier–Part Frequencies in Concept Context

However, both of these methods do not necessarily yield generally atypical modifiers that are however typical of a part when it is attributed to a specific concept. For example, birds' beaks are typically brown, orange or yellow, but aiming to extract modifiers for a crow's beak, *black* would be one of the desired modifiers – which does not appear at a high frequency rank as a generic beak modifier. The methods described so far did not take the concept into account when generating the modifier–part pairs, i. e., for all concepts with a specific part the same set of modifiers would be extracted.

To address this issue, a second frequency rank list was prepared in the same manner – with the only difference that the part noun had to appear within the context of the concept noun. That way, also modifiers for specific concepts' parts that deviate from the most typical part modifiers appear at a high rank. However, these data are sparser, which is why we used a wide context of 40 sentences (20 sentences before and after the part) within which the concept had to occur (i. e., a paragraph-like context size in which the topic, presumably, comprises the concept). We refer to ranked lists of modifier–part pairs that do not take the target concept into account as contextless lists, and to lists within the span of a context as in-context lists.

Due to the already mentioned data sparseness problem, not all modifiers used for a part noun in the production norms could be extracted with the latter method, as some of the obvious modifiers for specific parts are just not written about. For these, there is a higher chance that they appear, if at all, in the contextless rank list. For example, *thin bristles* does not appear in the context of *broom*. In the in-context list, 33% of the 229 triples extracted from the German norms were not found (in the contextless list, only 9% modifier–part pairs are missing). Additionally, particular concepts, parts, or concept–part pairs (within the 40 sentence span) might be missing from the corpus, as well. From the German norms collection, all concepts appeared in the corpus, but one part (a noun–noun compound), and 6 concept–part pairs (rare, colloquial part nouns) were missing. In the evaluation to follow, all the modifiers pertaining to these missing data from the corpus will be counted as positives not found by the algorithm.

	contextless		concept context	
rank	freq	modifier	freq	modifier
1	507	thick	16	thick
2	209	dense	14	white
3	204	soft	11	small
4	185	black	11	soft
5	175	long	9	dense

Table 1: Top 5 modifiers from frequency rank lists for part *fur* and concept *bear*

The example excerpt in table 1 shows modifiers that were selected for *bear* and *fur*, using the two frequency rank lists described above. Although in this example most of the modifiers (thick, dense, soft) are found in both lists, two arguably reasonable modifiers are just in the contextless set (black, long), and one only in the in-context set (white). A disadvantage of selecting modifiers from the in-context rank list is that many modifiers have the same low frequency, but they should nevertheless have differing ranks. In such cases, we assigned ranks according to alphabetic order of modifiers.

Summed Log-Rescaled Frequencies

Next, to improve performance and profit from both information sources the above methods provide, the in-context and contextless rank lists were combined. In one variant, the scaled frequencies for the concept–modifier–part triples appearing in both lists were added. Scaling was necessary because the frequencies in the contextless list are in general much higher than in the in-context list. Furthermore, to account for the fact that at high ranks the difference in frequency between subsequent ranks is much higher than at lower ranks, scaling was done by using the logarithmic values of the fre-

[3] Using the UCS toolkit, described at `http://www.collocations.de/software.html#UCS`

quencies: For each concept–modifier–part triple, its logarithmic frequency value was divided by the logarithmic value of the maximum corpus frequency of all parts in the corpus (in the contextless list) or of all concept–part pairs co-occurring within 40 sentences (in the case of the in-context list).

Productwise Combination of Frequencies

As an alternative back-off approach, the raw frequencies were combined productwise into a new list (for those modifier–part pairs missing in the in-context list, the frequency of the pair in the contextless list was taken alone, instead of multiplying it by zero; i. e., the in-context term was $\max(\text{freq}, 1)$). This achieves a sort of "intersective" effect, where modifiers that are both commonly attributed to the part and predicated of it in the context of the target concept are boosted up in the list, according to the intuition that a good modifier should be both plausible for the part in general, and typical for the concept at hand.

Cosine-Based Re-Ranking

An attempt to further improve performance is based on the idea that parts are described by some specific types of attributes. For example, a *leaf* would be characterised by its shape or consistency (e. g., *long*, *stiff*), whereas for *fur* rather colour should be considered (e. g., *white, brown*). If we are able to cluster modifiers for their attribute type and find out which attribute types are in particular important for a specific part, those could get a preference in the rank list and be moved towards the top. To approach this in a simple way, a re-ranking method is used which is supposed to cluster and choose the right cluster of modifiers implicitly: The modifiers in the (productwise-) combined list were tested for their similarity by looking if they co-occur with the same relative frequency with the same set of nouns. In case of high similarity (in this respect) of a modifier to a single other modifier, or if the modifier was similar to a lot of modifiers, it should be re-ranked to a higher position. In more detail, a vector was created for each modifier, denoting its co-occurrence frequencies with each noun in the corpus within a window of 4 tokens (on the left side of the noun). Random indexing helped to reduce the vector dimensionality from 27,345 to 3,000 elements (Sahlgren, 2005). These vectors served for calculating the cosine distances between modifiers. Then, for each of the top 200 modifiers in the combined frequency rank list (covering 84% of the triples from the German norms), the cosine distance was calculated to each of the top 100 modifiers in the contextless rank list. A constant of 1 was added to each of the computed cosines, thus obtaining a quantity between 1 and 2. The original combined frequency value was multiplied by this quantity (thus leaving it unchanged when the original cosine was 0, increasing it otherwise). From the re-ranked list resulting from this operation, we selected, again, the top 5 modifiers of each concept–part pair. For example, suppose that *black* is among the modifiers of a *crow*'s *beak* in the combined list. We compute the cosine similarity of *black* with the top 100 modifiers of *beak* (in any context), and, for each of these cosines, we multiply the original combined value of *black* by $\text{cosine}+1$. Since the colour is a common attribute of beaks, the presence of modifiers like *yellow* and *brown*, high on the contextless *beak* list, helps re-ranking *black* high in the *crow*-specific *beak* list. We hope that this method helps out concept-specific *values* (e. g., *black* for *crow*) of *attributes* that are in general typical of a part (*colour* for *beak*).

4.2 Performance on Composite Parts From the Production Norms

The feature norms data represented the gold standard for the evaluation of all sets of modifiers chosen by each of the described methods for the given concept–part pairs. Note that, even if a modifier–part pair was produced only once in the feature production norms, the corresponding concept–modifier–part triple was included in the gold standard – which contains 41 different concepts, 80 different parts, and 62 different modifiers, totalling to 229 concept–modifier–part triples. As in the German corpus there are 154,935 adjective–part-noun pairs, the random baseline (random guessing) for finding these 229 pairs is approaching 0 (similarly for Italian and the judgement dataset).

Figure 1 displays the performance of the methods on German in the form of a recall–precision graph. For each rank (1–5), overall recall and interpolated precision values are given for all modifier–part pairs up to this rank – note that precision at 1% recall is overrated as it is based on an arbitrary fraction of rank 1 pairs. As expected, extracting modifiers of parts within a concept context (the in-context list) achieves low recall. In contrast, modifiers that were extracted by querying the corpus for parts without considering the concept context have

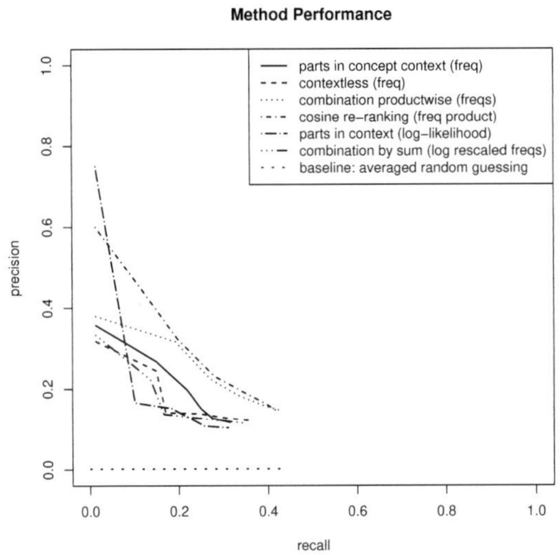

Figure 1: Evaluation on German norms

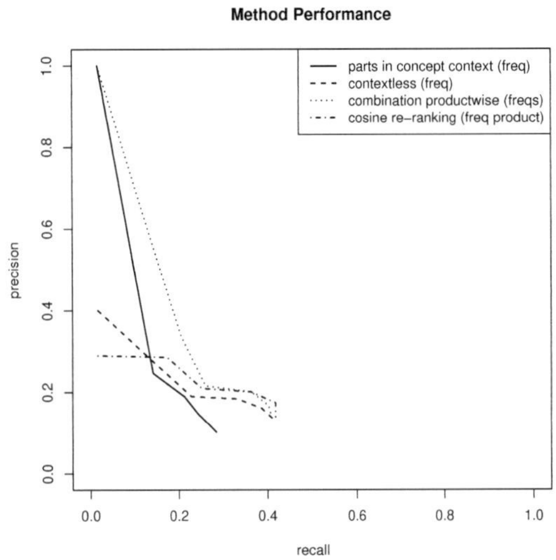

Figure 2: Evaluation on Italian norms

a higher recall. But this method has a lower precision in general. The performance for the method combining frequencies productwise and for the one that re-ranks this combined list via cosine-based smoothing are substantially better. Not only the precision is much higher at all recall levels, but also their maximum recall values are higher than those of the contextless lists, i. e., it was worth combining the complementing information in the two lists. However, the performance of the cosine-based re-ranked list compared to the productwise-combined list is not considerably higher, as we might have hoped. The remaining two alternative methods performed much worse: the one using log-likelihood values as ranking criterion had in general a low precision and a low recall, and the method combining the in-context and the contextless rank list by summing up the rescaled logarithmic frequency values performs as bad as the contextless rank list. Nevertheless, note that all methods perform distinctively well above the baseline.

Qualitatively analysing the data collected with the described methods did not give definite clues about why some performed not as good as expected. As a comprehensible example, the modifier *short* for *legs* is at rank 5 in the contextless list, but because of the frequent co-occurrence with *monkey* it rises to rank 2 in the productwise combination of these lists, and even to rank 1 in the cosine-based re-ranked list. An understandable bad performing example is the modifier *yellow* for the *eyes* of an *owl*: Although it appears in the in-context list at rank 2, it is a quite infrequent modifier for *eyes* in general (i. e., low in the contextless list), and thus it is not contained in the top 5 modifiers in the productwise combined rank list. On the other hand, it is not perfectly clear to us why, e. g., *flat* for the *roof* of a *skyscraper*, which is at rank 5 in the contextless list and at rank 6 in the combined list, is lowered to rank 9 in the cosine-based re-ranked list (in the in-context list, it does not appear at all). For all methods, collected modifiers include such of undesired attributes not describing the part, but other, rather situational aspects, e. g., *own*, *left*, *new*, *protecting*, and *famous*. Furthermore, we observed that some modifiers are reasonable for the respective concept–part pair, but they are counted as false because they did not occur in the production experiment (that we took as the evaluation basis), e. g., for the *blade* of a *sword*, not only *large* is acceptable, but also *long* and *wide*, essentially making the same assertion about the size of the *blade*. This issue is addressed further below by creating a new evaluation standard based on plausibility judgements.

To evaluate the cross-lingual performance of the extraction approach, the Italian norms were explored similarly to the German norms for composite parts. The gold standard here comprised 127 triples (from combinations of 30 different concepts, 45 parts, and 50 different modifiers). The same methods described above were used to extract modifiers from the Italian WaCky web corpus (more than 1.5 billion tokens), with one difference regarding the query for adjectives near nouns: As in the Italian language adjectives in a noun phrase can be used both before and after the noun (with differences in their meaning), and given that most of them were produced after the noun, we collected all adjectives occurring up to 2 words from the left of the noun and up to 4 words to the right.

Figure 2 shows the performance curves of the methods for the Italian data. In this evaluation, the method using log-likelihood values and the method combining lists via addition of logarithmic rescaled frequencies are omitted as their performance was not promising at all in the German data, and they are conceptually similar to the contextless and productwise-combination approaches, respectively. Like in German, the in-context method yields a low recall, in contrast to the method not considering the presence of concepts in context. Again, cosine-based re-ranking performs very similarly to the method using the productwise-combined list. For the performance on the Italian data, their difference from the simple frequency rank lists is not as large as it is for the German data, but it is clearly visible, especially at higher recall values.

Summarising, our comparison of various corpus-based ranking methods to the feature production norms, both in German and Italian, suggests that composite parts produced by subjects are best mined in corpora by making use of both general information about typical modifiers of the parts (the contextless rank) and more specific information about modifiers that co-occur with the part near the target concept. Moreover, it is better to combine the two information sources productwise, which suggests an intersecting effect (the most likely modifiers are both well-attested out of context and seen near the target concept). For both languages, there is no strong evidence that re-ranking by cosine similarity (a method that should favour modifiers that are values of common attributes of a part) is improving on the plain combination method (although re-ranking is not hurting, either).

By looking at the overall performance, the results are somewhat underwhelming, with precision around 20% at around 30% recall for the best models in both languages. A natural question at this point is whether the modifiers ranked at the top by the best methods and treated as false positives because they are not in the norms are nevertheless sensible modifiers for the parts, or whether they are truly noise. In order to explore this issue we turn now to our next experiment.

4.3 Performance Evaluation Based on Plausibility Judgements

The purpose of this judgement experiment was to see which concept–modifier–part triples the majority of participants would rate as acceptable. It allows us to investigate two topics: (i) the comparison of what people produce and what they perceive as being a prominent modifier for a concept–part pair (our algorithm might actually provide good candidates which were just not produced, as we just said) and (ii) a re-evaluation of the cosine-based re-ranking method (it could be in fact better than we thought because we only evaluated what was produced, but did not have a definite plausibility rating of the candidates missing in the norms).

The tested set contained the triples yielded by our two best performing methods (productwise combination and cosine-based re-ranking), which were applied to the German feature norms (692 triples, comprising 41 concepts and 71 parts). From this set, a set of triples was chosen randomly for each of the 46 participants (recruited by e-mail among acquaintances of the first author). The triples were presented to participants embedded into a natural-sounding sentence of the form "The [part] of a [concept] is [modifier]". Each participant rated 333 sentences, presented on separate lines of a text file (this set of sentences presented comprised additional triples which were intended for other purposes – for the current evaluation, we used a subset of 110 of these from each participant, on the average). Participants were instructed to read the sentences as general statements about a concept's part and mark them by typing a letter ("w" for wonderful and "d" for dubious – to facilitate one-handed typing and easy memorisation) at the beginning of the line, if they thought it plausible/unlikely that someone used the sentence to explain an aspect of the relevant part. In total, 5,525 judgements were collected; each sentence in the set was judged on the average by 8 persons.

The performance evaluation is based on the acceptance rate of the participants: Modifiers accepted by at least 75% of the raters are considered plausible. Figure 3 shows the recall–precision graph for the methods tested on the concept–part pairs from the German norms. From the 692 triples judged, around 13% were accepted by the majority of speakers. The precision rate is comparable with the evaluation on the basis of the modifiers produced by participants (highest recall is 1, of course,

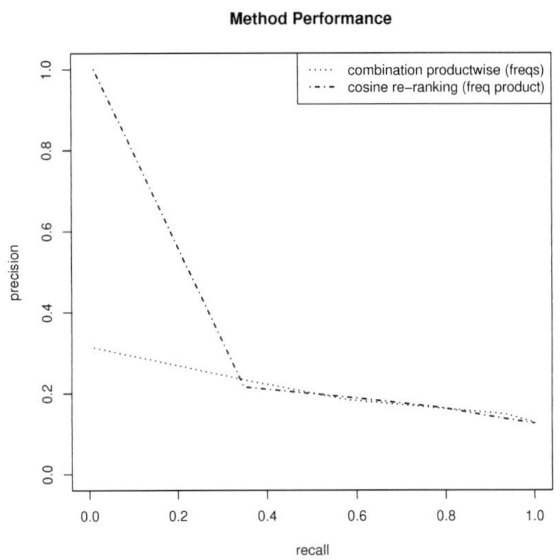

Figure 3: Evaluation on judgements (German)

because all modifiers to be judged were exclusively from the data set selected by our methods).

Again, the performance of the cosine-based re-ranking method is similar to the performance of the productwise-combination method. For a more exact evaluation of the difference between these two, a last test was conducted: Instead of measuring the performance in the form of counts of modifiers that were accepted by the majority of participants, we used the acceptance rates of all modifiers: The acceptance rates of all judged triples were summed up if they contained the same concept–part pair. This means that each concept–part pair received a score reflecting the overall acceptance of the set of modifiers for that pair (e. g., for *bear: fur*, all acceptance rates for *bear: brown fur*, *bear: soft fur*, ... were summed up). Then, the score of each concept–part pair in the productwise-combined list was compared against the score of the same pair for the cosine-based re-ranking method, using a pairwise t-test (this procedure is sound because the modifiers per pair are the same for the two methods). The test showed a significant difference ($p = 0.008$), but in favour of the productwise-combination method (score means were slightly higher). That is, cosine-based re-ranking in the current form brings no advantage over the simpler productwise combination of the frequency lists.

Finally, turning to the qualitative comparison of production and perception, there was a relatively small overlap of triples (46) contrasting with modifiers only produced but not accepted (53), and modifiers accepted but not produced (42). Intuitively, we would have expected that what was produced will be also accepted by the majority of people. Possibly, some participants in the judgement experiment found a few of the triples produced questionable (*goose: long beak*) – such triples were in our gold standard because we deliberately did not want to exclude composite parts even if produced by only one speaker – whereas participants producing parts for given concepts probably just did not think of specific parts or modifiers (e. g., *aeroplane: small windows* and *bear: dense fur*). The important fact regarding this difference is, however, that our method captures both kinds of modifiers.

5 Discussion

We presented several corpus-based methods that provide a set of adjective modifiers for each concrete concept–part pair, to be compared to those modifiers that are salient to human subjects. The general approach was to generate ranked lists, and select the 5 candidates at the top of the ranks.

The best of our methods works on the simple (productwise-) combination of frequency information of co-occurring adjective–noun pairs with and without considering a wide “concept context” in which the part noun has to occur. This method performed better than the one based on co-occurrence frequency not in concept context (generic modifiers, not appropriate for every concept) and the one based on co-occurrence frequencies in concept context, only (low recall because of sparse data).

We evaluated the methods on feature production norms and on plausibility judgements of generated concept–modifier–part triples to compare production and perception of modifiers. The performance was similar in precision – although the qualitative analysis showed that modifiers produced and modifiers perceived did not have a large overlap. This means our algorithm is capable of collecting both with the same performance.

After tuning the algorithm on German norms, we evaluated its generalisation capability to a different language (Italian). Performance was similar. Less satisfying at first glance is the precision value of just around 20% at the maximum recall level (however, when compared to the baseline of below 1% precision, this is an essentially better value) – as well as the fact that our implementation of the intuitive idea to re-rank modifiers that are similar (and should instantiate the same attribute) did not have a performance advantage. This is subject to further work. Moreover, using a machine-learning method (building a binary classifier) could be tried. Another idea was to crawl the web and select concept-specific text passages to build a specialised corpus. Possibly, we could draw then from a richer information source. A rough attempt to do this did not seem to yield promising results.

So far, we included only adjectives as permissible modifiers. A future extension could be also aiming for numerals (e. g., *four wheels*). Then, for the simulation of human-like behaviour we imagine as part of the possible future work to enable the algorithm to decide if a part noun should be paired with a modifier, at all – or if the part itself is sufficient to describe a concept (*big ears* vs. *trunk*).

Regarding the evaluation, a more exact performance measure would probably be achieved by either having more participants producing concept descriptions and then only selecting those modifiers for the gold standard that were produced by a majority – or letting participants in a judgement experiment also judge modifiers that were produced, to filter out the unlikely ones.

A next step in the project will be extracting salient parts for concepts (which we assumed to have done already for the purpose of this paper), possibly by integrating the information we already collected by extracting modifiers. In the end, we would like to come up with an adaptable method that extracts not only parts but also other types of relations (e. g., category, behaviour, function, etc.), which have been already addressed in related works, though. The issue we presented in this paper, however, is new and, we think, worth exploring.

References

Abdulrahman Almuhareb. 2006. *Attributes in Lexical Acquisition*. Phd thesis, University of Essex.

Mark Andrews, Gabriella Vigliocco, and David Vinson. 2009. Integrating experiential and distributional data to learn semantic representations. *Psychological Review*, 116(3):463–498.

Marco Baroni, Eduard Barbu, Brian Murphy, and Massimo Poesio. 2010. Strudel: A distributional semantic model based on properties and types. *Cognitive Science*, 34(2):222–254.

Kenneth Church and Peter Hanks. 1990. Word association norms, mutual information, and lexicography. *Computational Linguistics*, 16(1):22–29.

Stefan Evert. 2008. Corpora and collocations. In A. Lüdeling and M. Kytö, editors, *Corpus Linguistics: An International Handbook*, pages 1212–1248. Mouton de Gruyter, Berlin, Germany.

Christiane Fellbaum, editor. 1998. *WordNet: An Electronic Lexical Database*. MIT Press, Cambridge, MA.

Nikesh Garera and David Yarowsky. 2009. Structural, transitive and latent models for biographic fact extraction. In *Proceedings of EACL*, pages 300–308, Athens, Greece.

Peter Garrard, Matthew Lambon Ralph, John Hodges, and Karalyn Patterson. 2001. Prototypicality, distinctiveness, and intercorrelation: Analyses of the semantic attributes of living and nonliving concepts. *Cognitive Neuropsychology*, 18(2):25–174.

Roxana Girju, Adriana Badulescu, and Dan Moldovan. 2006. Automatic discovery of part-whole relations. *Computational Linguistics*, 32(1):83–135.

Marti Hearst. 1992. Automatic acquisition of hyponyms from large text corpora. In *Proceedings of COLING*, pages 539–545, Nantes, France.

Gerhard Kremer, Andrea Abel, and Marco Baroni. 2008. Cognitively salient relations for multilingual lexicography. In *Proceedings of the COGALEX Workshop at COLING08*, pages 94–101.

Hugo Liu and Push Singh. 2004. ConceptNet: A practical commonsense reasoning toolkit. *BT Technology Journal*, pages 211–226.

Ken McRae, George Cree, Mark Seidenberg, and Chris McNorgan. 2005. Semantic feature production norms for a large set of living and nonliving things. *Behavior Research Methods*, 37(4):547–559.

Patrick Pantel and Marco Pennacchiotti. 2006. Espresso: Leveraging generic patterns for automatically harvesting semantic relations. In *Proceedings of COLING-ACL*, pages 113–120, Sydney, Australia.

Magnus Sahlgren. 2005. An introduction to random indexing. `http://www.sics.se/~mange/papers/RI_intro.pdf`.

Cyrus Shaoul and Chris Westbury. 2008. Performance of HAL-like word space models on semantic clustering. In *Proceedings of the ESSLLI Workshop on Distributional Lexical Semantics*, pages 42–46, Hamburg, Germany.

Donald Spence and Kimberly Owens. 1990. Lexical co-occurrence and association strength. *Journal of Psycholinguistic Research*, 19(5):317–330.

David Vinson and Gabriella Vigliocco. 2008. Semantic feature production norms for a large set of objects and events. *Behavior Research Methods*, 40(1):183–190.

Towards a Data-Driven Model of Eye Movement Control in Reading

Mattias Nilsson
Department of Linguistics and Philology
Uppsala University
mattias.nilsson@lingfil.uu.se

Joakim Nivre
Department of Linguistics and Philology
Uppsala University
joakim.nivre@lingfil.uu.se

Abstract

This paper presents a data-driven model of eye movement control in reading that builds on earlier work using machine learning methods to model saccade behavior. We extend previous work by modeling the time course of eye movements, in addition to where the eyes move. In this model, the initiation of eye movements is delayed as a function of on-line processing difficulty, and the decision of where to move the eyes is guided by past reading experience, approximated using machine learning methods. In benchmarking the model against held-out previously unseen data, we show that it can predict gaze durations and skipping probabilities with good accuracy.

1 Introduction

Eye movements during reading proceed as an alternating series of fixations and saccades with considerable variability in fixation times and saccade lengths. This variation reflects, at least to some extent, language-related processes during reading. Much psycholinguistic research, therefore, relies on measures of eye movements in reading to gain an understanding of human sentence processing. Eye tracking recordings are routinely used to study how readers' eye movements respond to experimental manipulation of linguistic stimuli (Clifton et al., 2007), and corpus-based analysis of eye-tracking data has recently emerged as a new way to evaluate theories of human sentence processing difficulty (Boston et al., 2008; Demberg and Keller, 2008).

More detailed accounts of the workings of the eye movement system during reading are offered by computational models of eye movement control (see Reichle (2006b), for an overview of recent models). These models receive text as input and produce predictions for the placement and duration of fixations, in approximation to human reading behavior. Because eye movements in reading rely on a coupled cognitive-motor system, such models provide detailed accounts for how eye movements are controlled both by on-line language processing and lower-level motor control. Current models such as E-Z Reader (Reichle, 2006a; Pollatsek et al., 2006; Reichle et al., 2009) and SWIFT (Engbert et al., 2002; Engbert et al., 2005) account for numerous of the known facts about saccade behavior in reading. This includes word frequency and predictability effects on fixation times, word skipping rates, and preview and spillover effects.

A recent approach to eye-movement modeling, less tied to psychophysiological assumptions about the mechanisms that drive eye movements, is to build models directly from eye-tracking data using machine learning techniques inspired by recent work in natural language processing. Thus, Nilsson and Nivre (2009) show how a classifier can be trained on authentic eye-tracking data and then used to predict the saccade behavior of individual readers on new texts. Methodologically this differs from the standard approach in computational modeling of eye movement control, where model parameters are often fitted to data but model predictions are not evaluated on unseen data in order to assess the generalization error of these predictions. Without questioning the validity of the standard approach, we believe that the strict separation of training data and test data assumed in machine learning may provide additional insights about the properties of these models.

The model of Nilsson and Nivre (2009) is based on a simple transition system for saccadic movements, a classifier that predicts where to fixate next and a classifier-guided search algorithm to simulate fixation sequences over sentences.

Proceedings of the 2010 Workshop on Cognitive Modeling and Computational Linguistics, ACL 2010, pages 63–71,
Uppsala, Sweden, 15 July 2010.

One obvious limitation of the model proposed by Nilsson and Nivre (2009) is that it does not at all capture the temporal aspects of eye movement behavior. Thus, for example, it says nothing about when eye movements are initiated or when the decision of where to fixate next is made during fixations. In this paper, we try to overcome this limitation by placing the machine-learning approach in a broader psychological context and detail a model that also accounts for the timing of fixations. More precisely, we present a model of the time course of eye movements, where saccade timing is driven by on-line language processing and where-decisions are driven by the experience readers have built up through years of reading practice.[1]

It is not our intention in this paper to present a full-fledged model of eye movement control in reading. The model is limited in scope and does not address certain important aspects of eye movement control, such as within-word fixation locations, refixations and regressions triggered by higher-order processing. In addition, the linguistic features influencing timing (when-decisions) and target selection (where-decisions) are restricted to the basic variables word length and frequency. In this way, we hope to provide a baseline against which richer models of language processing can be evaluated.

The rest of this paper is structured as follows. Section 2 provides a brief background on what is known about the time course of eye movements during reading. Here we introduce some common notions that will be used later on. In section 3, we first give an overview of the model and then describe its component processes and how these processes interrelate. In section 4, we present an experimental evaluation of the model using data from the English section of the Dundee corpus (Kennedy and Pynte, 2005). Section 5 contains our conclusions and suggestions for future research.

2 The Timing of Eye Movements

The average fixation duration in reading is about 250 ms, and most fixations last between 200-300 ms, although they may range from under 100 ms to over 500 ms for a given reader (Rayner, 1998). Because eye movements are a motor response requiring preparation before execution, they are initiated well before the end of the fixation. Hence, there is a *saccade latency* of about 150-200 ms from the time when a saccade is first initiated until the eye movement is actually executed (Becker and Jürgens, 1979; McPeek et al., 2000). Once the eye movement is executed, it takes about 25-45 ms before the eyes are fixated on a new word again, depending on the length of the movement.

Given an average saccade latency of about 150-200 ms, and an average fixation duration of 250 ms, it seems clear that eye movements are often initiated within the first 100 ms of a fixation. However, as Reichle notes (Reichle et al., 2003), since the time it takes to identify words is on the order of 150 - 300 ms, this suggests that there is not enough time for language processes to have any direct on-line influence on eye movements. One key observation to explain language influences on eye movements, however, is the finding that readers often start processing upcoming words before they are fixated. Studies on *parafoveal preview* show that the amount of time spent fixating a word depends, among other things, on how much parafoveal preview of the word is available prior to the word being fixated (Balota et al., 1985; Pollatsek et al., 1992).

A further finding supporting the assumption that language processes can have an early effect on eye movements comes from the disappearing text studies (Rayner et al., 1981; Rayner et al., 2003). In these studies, words become masked or disappear at a certain point during the fixation. Despite this, a word need only be on display for 50-60 ms in order for reading to proceed quite normally. More importantly, the time the eyes remain fixated after a word disappears depends on the frequency of the word. Readers remain fixated on low-frequency words longer than on high-frequency words, even though the word that was fixated has actually disappeared. In summary, these studies suggest that there is a robust word frequency effect in reading as early as 60 ms after the onset of the fixation.

3 A Model of Eye Movement Control

3.1 General Overview

The model we develop takes the basic time constraints associated with language processing and motor control as a starting point. This means that our model is driven by estimates of the time it

[1] This view of where-decisions being driven by experience is similar in spirit to some earlier theories of saccade target selection in reading, such as the probabilistic account of word skipping proposed by Brysbaert and Vitu (1998).

takes to process words, plan an eye movement, execute a saccade etc. In line with cognitive control models of eye movements in reading, such as E-Z Reader, we assume that the cognitive processing of words is the "engine" that drives eye movements. That is, eye movements are initiated in response to on-line language processing. Unlike E-Z Reader, however, we do not presume a two-stage lexical process where the completion of a certain hypothesized first stage triggers an eye movement.[2] Instead, when the eyes move to a new word, an eye movement is initiated after some delay that is proportional to the amount of cognitive work left on the word. Furthermore, in contrast to E-Z Reader we assume that saccade initiation is decoupled from the decision of where to move the eyes. In E-Z Reader, the initiation of a saccade program is in effect a decision to start programming a saccade to the next word. Here, instead, the target for the next saccade can be any of the words in the forward perceptual span. Another related difference, with respect to previous cognitive control models, is that we assume that the decision of where to move the eyes is not directly influenced by on-line language processing. Instead, this decision is governed by an autonomous routine, having its own dynamics automated through years of reading experience. This experience is approximated using machine learning methods on authentic eye tracking data.

The model is defined in terms of four processes that we assume are operative during reading: lexical processing (*L*), saccade initiation delay (*D*), motor programming (*M*), and saccade execution (*S*). These processes are defined in terms of a set of parameters that determine their duration. Once an ongoing process ends, a subsequent process is initiated, for as long as reading continues. As is commonly assumed in most models of eye movement control, language-related processes and motor control processes can run in parallel. We will use the notation w_i to refer to the ith word in a text $w_1, \ldots, w_n$ consisting of n words, and we will use subscripted symbols L_i, D_i, M_i and S_i to refer to the lexical processing, the saccade initiation delay, the motor programming, and the saccade execution associated with w_i.

In the following four subsections, we outline these processes in detail and discuss the general assumptions underlying them. We then conclude this section by summarizing how the processes dynamically interact to produce eye movement behavior.

3.2 Lexical Processing

The time needed to process individual words in reading is certain to depend on numerous factors related to a person's prior reading experience, word-level properties such as length and frequency, and higher-order language processes such as syntactic and semantic processing. However, since our goal in this paper is to validate a simple model, with as few parameters as possible, we make the simplifying assumption that the processing time of a word can be approximated by its length (number of characters) and its frequency of occurrence in printed text. In particular, we assume that the mean time required for processing a word w_i is a linear function of its length and the natural logarithm of its frequency:[3]

$$t(L_i) = b_0 + b_1 \,\text{length}(w_i) - b_2 \,\ln(\text{freq}(w_i)) \quad (1)$$

In equation 1, b_0 is the intercept representing the base time needed to process a word while b_1 and b_2 are the respective slopes for the effect of length and frequency on the base processing time. Again, we stress that equation 1 is by all accounts an oversimplification. Thus, for example, it does not take into account any higher-level top-down influence on processing time.

Still, we believe equation 1 provides a reasonable first approximation. A large part of the variance in measures of reading time can be accounted for by word frequency and word length. At any rate, our simple assumption with respect to processing time represents a methodological decision rather than a theoretical one. We want to keep the model as simple as possible at this stage, and later explore the effect of including variables related to higher-order processing.

Once the time interval $t(L_i)$ has passed for a given word w_i, lexical processing begins on the next word. Thus, the completion of $t(L_i)$ results in the initiation of L_{i+1}. Because the processing of the next word does not start until the processing of the current word is finished, lexical processing

[2] In E-Z Reader, the first stage of lexical processing is an early estimate of the word's familiarity that provides the signal to the eye movement system that lexical access is imminent and that a saccade should be planned.

[3] We use the logarithm of word frequency because human response times, in lexical decision tasks for instance, are linearly related to the natural logarithm of word frequency (Balota and Chumbley, 1984).

proceeds serially and no more than one word is processed at any given time.

3.3 Saccade Initiation Delay

When the eyes move to a new word w_i, a motor program is initiated after some time. We assume that the time when a motor program is initiated depends on the processing difficulty of the fixated word w_i. In particular, the signal to initiate a saccade is deferred in proportion to how much processing remains on w_i, or put differently, in proportion to how much work remains to be done on that word. This general routine serves to prevent the control system from making over-hasty saccades to new words. The length of the saccade initiation delay $t(D)$ is proportional to the remaining processing time of word w_i at fixation onset:

$$t(D_i) = d\,(t(L_i) - t(E_i)) \qquad (2)$$

where d is a free parameter representing a proportion, $t(L_i)$ is the lexical processing time for the fixated word, and $t(E_i)$ denotes the interval of time that has elapsed since the initiation of $t(L_i)$. More difficult words are associated with longer processing times and thus cause later initiation of saccade programs and therefore also longer fixation durations. The free parameter d defines a proportion taking values in the range $[0, 1]$. The extremes of this range can be interpreted as follows. If d is set equal to 0, a new saccade program is initiated immediately upon a new fixation. If d instead is set equal to 1, the saccade program starts only after the fixated word has been fully processed. More generally, a change of the value of this parameter can be understood as a change of the amount of cognitive influence on fixation durations. The higher its value, the more cognitive work must be carried out before a new saccade program is started. Once the time interval $t(D)$ has passed, the planning of a new eye movement starts, i.e., a motor program, M, is initiated.

3.4 Motor Programming

The time needed to plan and initiate an eye movement defines the saccade latency, or motor programming time $t(M)$. We assume that the duration of this period is given by the free parameter m:

$$t(M_i) = m \qquad (3)$$

The following is worth noting. Some influential research suggests that motor programming is completed in two stages (Becker and Jürgens, 1979). The first of these being a labile stage during which a planned saccade can be canceled, e.g., in favor of another saccade target. The second stage, closer in time to the execution of the saccade, is non-labile and once entered, a saccade underway can no longer be modified or canceled. This division between labile and non-labile stages of motor programming is sometimes implemented in computational models, for example in E-Z Reader and SWIFT. For now, however, our model does not operationalize the notion of saccade canceling and thus makes no useful distinction between labile and non-labile stages of motor programming. Our only assumption with respect to these different stages of motor programming is that their respective durations sum up to m.

An important function of motor programming in our model, however, is to select a target for the saccade. Before discussing how this is achieved we should point out that we make no claim as to how much time of motor programming is consumed by target selection. It is only presupposed that saccade target selection, in the normal course of events, is initiated as soon as there is a decision to make an eye movement (i.e., when motor programming starts), and that, whatever time remains of motor programming once a target is selected, this time is spent on preparation of the physical movement to the selected target. Once motor programming is finished, a saccade S is executed to the target.

Following Nilsson and Nivre (2009), we treat target selection as a classification task. In practical terms, this means that we train a classifier to predict the most likely eye movement following any fixation. An instance to be classified consists of a feature vector encoding feature information over the current fixated word and words in the immediate context. Given such feature representations and training data obtained from eye-tracking recordings, essentially any standard machine learning algorithm can be applied to the classification task. The type of learning algorithm that performs best on this task is, however, unknown. Rather than speculate, we suggest that this is a question for further research.

The remaining assumptions we make are as follows. First, because there is a sharp drop-off in acuity of the human eye around the point of fixation, the number of words that can be discriminated in parafoveal vision on a given fixation is limited to a few. Therefore, it is reasonable to assume that the potential targets for a saccade on any given fixation are limited to the words available within the range of effective vision. [4] This is supported empirically by the fact that the great majority of outgoing saccades tend to land in one of the three words that follow the current fixation. Moreover, we assume that for these potential targets, only rather coarse, visual information, such as a gross appreciation of their length, can be extracted on any given fixation. The reason for this is that target selection generally occurs relatively early on in a fixation, at a time when only low-level visual information can reasonably be gleaned from the parafovea.

Secondly, we reason that target selection reflects an autonomous process that has been automated, through years of practice, to *progress* through the text and select targets in the default reading direction. Hence, the possible targets for target selection, as construed here, is limited to the targets within the forward field of effective vision. As a consequence, words to the left of the current fixation are not fixated as a result of target selection.

Finally, we assume that target selection by default is a mechanical routine, insensitive to ongoing lexical processing. In the general case, then, the decision of where to move eyes is made independently of processing considerations. Motor programs in general, however, may sometimes override the default target selection mechanism and be initiated, not in order to *select* a new target, but to *correct* for situations where motor control and ongoing language processing are threatening to desynchronize. Such a corrective program may be initiated, for instance, if a saccade is executed to word_i but lexical processing has not yet completed on word_{i-1}, and so more lexical processing of word_{i-1} is needed before moving on. In this case, a corrective motor program is initiated to word_{i-1}, subsequently resulting in a regression to that word. In this way, corrective motor programs serve to synchronize the eyes with the current processing stream and for that reason they always target the word being processed. Moreover, because corrective saccade programs are launched with a fixed target, they do not trigger target selection during motor programming.

[4]The effective visual field (the perceptual span) extends about four characters to the left and 15 characters to the right of the fixation for normal readers of left-to-right orthographies (Rayner, 1998).

3.5 Saccade Execution

The time to execute a saccade $t(S)$ is determined by the free parameter s:

$$t(S_i) = s \tag{4}$$

Once a saccade has been executed, the position of the eyes shifts to a new word and thus, in the normal course of events, a new motor program is initiated after $t(D_i)$. However, sometimes a saccade is made ahead of the current processing stream, because, as noted earlier, a word needs not be fully processed before a saccade is executed to another word. Likewise, a saccade may sometimes be executed to a word that has already been fully processed, because target selection is an autonomous process, not influenced by ongoing processing. In these situations, corrective saccade programs are initiated. Since corrective saccade programs serve only to rapidly coordinate the eyes and the current processing stream, we assume that they can be initiated immediately and hence that they are not subject to saccade initiation delay.

3.6 Eye Movement Control

Having defined the respective component processes, we now consider how these processes are coordinated to model eye movement control. Lexical processing is always running in parallel with the processes controlling saccade initiation delay, motor programming and saccade execution, which are executed in sequence. A simulation of reading is started by initiating lexical processing of the first word (L_1), and the saccade initiation delay for the first word (D_1) (i.e., the first word is fixated). Whenever one of the running processes terminates, new processes are initiated in the following way:

- If L_i terminates, initiate L_{i+1}.
- If D_i terminates, initiate M_i and select new fixation target w_j.
- If M_i terminates, initiate S_i.
- If S_i terminates and the ongoing lexical process is L_j:
  - If $i = j$, initiate D_i.
  - If $i \neq j$, initiate M_j and set fixation target to w_j

The simulation terminates when all words have been lexically processed.

4 Experimental Evaluation

4.1 Experimental Setup

In order to estimate the performance of the model described in the previous section, some experiments were performed using data from the English section of the Dundee corpus (Kennedy and Pynte, 2005).

In most evaluations of eye movement control models, the model parameters are fitted against one and the same corpus by searching the parameter space to find the set of parameter values that best simulates the observed data. This approach makes it somewhat hard to appreciate how well a given model generalizes to new, previously unseen data. A more stringent evaluation, which affords an assessment of the generalization error of model predictions, is to set the model parameters on some portion of the data and then test the model on another held-out portion. The results we report in this paper were obtained this way.

The Dundee corpus that was used in these experiments contains the eye tracking records of ten subjects reading editorials from The Independent, a UK broadsheet newspaper. The data consist of 20 texts that were read by all subjects, and close to 2400 sentences. We divided these texts into three sets: the first 16 for training (1911 sentences), 17-18 for model development and validation (237 sentences), and the last two texts, 19-20, for blind testing of the model (231 sentences). Model parameters were fitted using only the training and validation set, prior to evaluating the model on the held-out test set.

Next we discuss how training was performed, both in terms of the training of the classifier for target selection and in terms of the estimation of the model's process parameters on the training data. Before presenting the results, we also discuss some standard practice in benchmarking models of eye movement control.

4.2 Training the Classifier

We used the transition-based model outlined by Nilsson and Nivre (2009) in combination with logistic regression for training the target selection classifier. The classifier was trained on a restricted number of features defined over words in the fixation context. The feature model we used for these experiments included information about the word length of the current fixation and upcoming words, as well as some historical information about recently made eye movements. The history of previous eye movements was represented in terms of the saccade distance (measured in number of words) that led up to recently made fixations (including the current fixation). In this way, the feature model contained information about, for instance, whether the saccade that led up to the current fixation skipped a word or two.

In contrast to Nilsson and Nivre (2009) we did not train one model for each individual subject in the corpus. Instead, we trained a single multiple-subject classifier on all ten readers in the training set. The performance of this classifier was assessed in terms of how well, on average, it predicted the observed saccade targets for any given reader on the development set. Moreover, in line with the assumption that target selection is restricted to a limited number of candidate words in the forward visual field, the classifier was trained to select one of the three words following any fixation as the target for a saccade. This cross-subject classifier achieved an average prediction accuracy of 72% on the development set.

4.3 Estimating Model Parameters

Because the model's process parameters can not be directly estimated from eye tracking data they need to be approximated in other ways. The values for the intercept and slope parameters for lexical processing time $t(L_i)$ were obtained by fitting a linear regression of gaze duration on logarithmic word frequency and word length on the training data. The assumption that the gaze duration on a given word reflects the time required to process the word is necessarily an oversimplification but is sometimes used in eye movement modeling. A number of studies indicate that it is indeed a reasonable approximation (Engbert et al., 2002; Pollatsek et al., 2006).

The value for the parameter d in the equation for $t(D_i)$ was selected based on a simple parameter search over the training data. The best fitting value was assessed by calculating the root mean square error between predicted and observed values for gaze durations for different values of d ranging from 0 to 1 in 0.1 increments, while keeping other parameter values unchanged. To keep things simple, the parameters that determine the mean duration of motor programming, m, and saccade execution, s, were fixed at 200 ms, and 25 ms, respectively. These values are in good agreement with

Parameter	Interpretation	Value
b_0	Intercept: base lexical processing time (ms)	165.5
b_1	Slope: effect of length on lexical processing time (ms)	13.5
b_2	Slope: effect of frequency on lexical processing time (ms)	3.2
d	Proportion of lexical processing time (determines saccade initiation delay)	0.5
m	Mean motor programming time (ms)	200
s	Mean saccade execution time (ms)	25

Table 1: Model parameters, their interpretations and values, as estimated during training.

estimated values in experimental studies. Table 1 lists the model's six process parameters and their values, obtained prior to testing the model.

4.4 Benchmark Evaluation

Models of eye movement control in reading are typically benchmarked against a set of word-based dependent eye movement measures which are averaged across subjects. Two such measures are gaze duration and probability of skipping. Gaze duration is defined as the sum duration of all fixations on a word prior to any saccade leaving the word during first-pass reading. Probability of skipping is simply the mean probability (across subjects) that a given word is skipped (not fixated) during first-pass reading.

Because word frequency effects on eye movements during reading are robust and well-documented, one common benchmark practice is to evaluate models with respect to their capability of reproducing word frequency effects on fixation times and fixation probabilities. Typically, averages of word-based measures are then broken down into word-frequency classes. This is a fairly simple way to see how well a given model can predict observed means for measures such as gaze duration and skipping probability for words of different frequency classes. The results we report are presented this way. We used frequency estimates based on word occurrences in the written part of the British National Corpus (BNC). Frequencies were normalized to occurrences per million words and then divided into five frequency classes, as suggested by Reichle et al. (1998).

In addition to the model we have outlined so far, we also present results for two alternative versions. These models differ from the one we have discussed only in positing a simpler function for lexical processing time. The alternative versions model lexical processing time only as a linear function of either word length or logarithmic word frequency. Hence, we fitted two separate simple linear regressions of gaze duration first on word length, and then on logarithmic word frequency. The regression coefficient and slope were estimated to 132.5 and 16 for the model based on word length, and 284 and -11 for the model based on frequency.

4.5 Results and Discussion

Table 2 shows the observed (empirical) and predicted (simulated) values of gaze durations and skipping probabilities for each of the five word frequency classes, both on the development set and on the held-out test set. M_1 and M_2 represent the versions of the model in which lexical processing time is a linear function of word length, and word frequency, respectively. M_3 represents the version of the model where lexical processing time is a linear function of both variables.

The results show that all three models, on the development set as well as on the test set, are able to reproduce the most important aspect of the observed data, namely, that mean gaze durations decrease and mean skipping probabilities increase with increasing word frequency. Overall, M_3 performs better than the two other models in predicting this relationship. The model based only on word length, M_1, performs worse than the other two models. This is mainly due to the poor performance of this model in simulating the proportions of skipped words in the upper frequency classes 4 and 5. In comparison to both M_2 and M_3, M_1 seriously underestimates the observed skipping probability for words belonging to these frequency classes, on both development and test data.

With respect to gaze duration alone, the three models perform similarly, although M_3 provides a somewhat better fit on both data sets. The models generally predict longer gaze durations than the observed means, except for the most low-frequent words. In particular, gaze durations for higher-frequency words (class 4 and 5) are prolonged compared to the means, giving an overall nar-

	Gaze duration								Probability of skipping							
	Development				Test				Development				Test			
Frequency class	Observed	M_1	M_2	M_3	Observed	M_1	M_2	M_3	Observed	M_1	M_2	M_3	Observed	M_1	M_2	M_3
1	290	282	280	285	286	278	280	284	0.17	0.15	0.18	0.13	0.16	0.14	0.19	0.14
2	257	271	259	272	261	273	260	275	0.19	0.18	0.20	0.16	0.19	0.15	0.22	0.17
3	229	254	252	249	235	257	254	252	0.24	0.19	0.24	0.20	0.22	0.19	0.25	0.20
4	208	240	238	237	210	244	238	237	0.52	0.23	0.36	0.43	0.53	0.24	0.34	0.40
5	198	238	236	228	195	239	237	230	0.65	0.34	0.51	0.54	0.67	0.32	0.52	0.51

Table 2: Observed and predicted values of Gaze Durations (ms) and Skipping Probabilities on development and test set for five frequency classes of words. M_1: $t(L_i) = b_0 + b_1\text{length}(w_i)$, Root mean square error on development set = 0.48, Root mean square error on test set = 0.52; M_2: $t(L_i) = b_0 - b_1 \ln(\text{freq}(w_i))$, Root mean square error on development set = 0.33, Root mean square error on test set = 0.35; M_3: $t(L_i) = b_0 + b_1\text{length}(w_i) - b_2 \ln(\text{freq}(w_i))$, Root mean square error on development set = 0.21, Root mean square error on test set = 0.26; Frequency range: 1:1-10, 2:11-100, 3:101-1000, 4:1001-10000, 5: 10001+

rower range of mean values for the five frequency classes.

The overall performance of each model, M_1, M_2 and M_3 was estimated by calculating the root mean square error (RMSE) between the mean observed and predicted gaze durations and probabilities of skipping. The errors were normalized as described in Reichle et al. (1998). In comparing the results for both development and test data, the best overall fit is provided by M_3 on the development set, giving an RMSE of 0.21 (smaller values indicate better fit). The fit for the same model drops to 0.26 when evaluated on the held-out test data.

To provide some basis for comparison, the earliest version of E-Z Reader (Reichle et al., 1998) which was fitted to the same dependent measures, had an RMSE of 0.145. It is important to point out, however, that this result was based on fitting the model parameters to a single sentence corpus of 48 sentences designed for experimental purposes. This corpus contained relatively short (8-14 words) isolated sentences without any connecting discourse. More generally, as noted by Reichle et al. (2009), RMSD values lower than 0.5 provide fits that are reasonably close to the observed means. By this standard, the model M_3 performs rather well in simulating the observed data. Moreover, this version of the model provides the most realistic estimates of the time it takes to identify words. Thus, for example, the mean time to identify the most frequent word in English, "the" (frequency class 5), is estimated to be 171 ms, whereas the mean time to identify the word "repopulate", which is a low-frequency (frequency class 1) ten-letter word is estimated to be 301 ms. These estimates are in good agreement with experimental estimates, which show that word identification latencies range between 150 and 300 ms (Rayner and Pollatsek, 1989).

5 Conclusion

In this paper we built on previous work using machine learning methods to model saccade behavior in reading and we extended this work by presenting a data-driven model of eye movement control that provides detailed predictions for both *when* and *where* the eyes move during reading. The most important principles of this model are *(i)* the initiation of eye movements is delayed as a function of on-line processing difficulty, and *(ii)* the decision of where to move the eyes is driven by an autonomous routine that has become automated through years of practice in reading. The model was trained on eye movements made over a large corpus of natural text. In benchmarking the model against held-out data we showed that it is able to reproduce frequency effects on both gaze duration and skipping probability with good accuracy (RMSE = 0.26).

Looking ahead, we plan to extend the model to account for more empirical data on eye movement behavior in reading. One important step to meet this goal is to develop a more informed model of language processing. Current models of eye movement control in reading generally assume that influences from syntactic and higher-order processing occur too late in the processing stream to directly influence eye movements. This is, however, seemingly at odds with recent findings in sentence processing research showing an influence of syntactic processing difficulty on both early and late measures of eye movements in reading (Demberg and Keller, 2008; Boston et al., 2008). Hence, it is possible that a more accurate model of eye movements in reading will need to allow for syntactic processing to influence the early decisions that control the timing of eye movements. This and other issues will be addressed in future work.

References

David. A Balota and James. I Chumbley. 1984. Are lexical decisions a good measure of lexical access? the role of word frequency in the neglected decision stage. *Journal of Experimental Psychology: Human perception and Performace*, 10:340–357.

David. A. Balota, Alexander Pollatsek, and Keith Rayner. 1985. The interaction of contextual constraints and parafoveal visual information in reading. *Cognitive Psychology*, 17:364–390.

W Becker and R Jürgens. 1979. An analysis of the saccadic system by means of double step stimuli. *Vision Research*, 19:967–983.

Marisa F. Boston, John Hale, Reinhold Kliegl, Umesh Patil, and Shravan Vasishth. 2008. Parsing costs as predictors of reading difficulty: An evaluation using the potsdam sentence corpus. *Journal of Eye Movement Reasearch*, 2:1–12.

Marc Brysbaert and Françoise Vitu. 1998. Word skipping: implications for theories of eye movement control in reading. In Geoffrey Underwood, editor, *Eye guidance in Reading and Scene Perception*, pages 124–147. Elsevier science Ltd.

Charles Clifton, Adrian Staub, and Keith Rayner. 2007. Eye movements in reading words and sentences. In Roger van Gompel, editor, *Eye movements: A window on mind and brain*, pages 341–372. Amsterdam: Elsevier.

Vera Demberg and Frank Keller. 2008. Data from eye-tracking corpora as evidence for theories of syntactic processing complexity. *Cognition*, 109:193–210.

Ralf Engbert, André Longtin, and Reinhold Kliegl. 2002. A dynamical model of saccade generation in reading based on spatially distributed lexical processing. *Vision Research*, 42:621–636.

Ralf Engbert, Antje Nuthmann, Eike Richter, and Reinhold Kliegl. 2005. SWIFT: A dynamical model of saccade generation during reading. *Psychological Review*, 112:777–813.

Alan Kennedy and Joël Pynte. 2005. Parafoveal-on-foveal effects in normal reading. *Vision research*, 45:153–168.

R. M. McPeek, A. A. Skavenski, and K Nakayama. 2000. Concurrent processing of saccades in visual search. *Vision Research*, 40:2499–2516.

Mattias Nilsson and Joakim Nivre. 2009. Learning where to look: Modeling eye movements in reading. In *Proceedings of the Thirteenth Conference on Computational Natural Language Learning (CoNLL-2009)*, pages 93–101.

Alexander Pollatsek, Mary Lesch, Robin K. Morris, and Keith Rayner. 1992. Phonological codes are used in integrating information across saccades in word identification and reading. *Experimental Psychology: Human Perception and Performance*, 18:148–162.

Alexander Pollatsek, Erik Reichle, and Keith Rayner. 2006. Tests of the E-Z Reader model: Exploring the interface between cognition and eye movements. *Cognitive Psychology*, 52:1–56.

Keith Rayner and Alexander Pollatsek. 1989. *The psychology of reading*. Englewood Cliffs, NJ: Prentice Hall.

Keith Rayner, Albert W. Inhoff, Robert E. Morrison, Maria L. Slowiaczek, and James H. Bertera. 1981. Masking of foveal and parafoveal vision during eye fixations in reading. *Journal of Experimental Psychology: Human Perception and Performance*, 7:167–179.

Keith Rayner, Simon P. Liversedge, Sarah J. White, and Dorine Vergilino-Perez. 2003. Reading disappearing text: cognitive control of eye movements. *Psychological science*, 14:385–388.

Keith Rayner. 1998. Eye movements in reading and information processing: 20 years of research. *Psychological Bulletin*, 124:372–422.

Erik Reichle, Alexander Pollatsek, Donald Fisher, and Keith Rayner. 1998. Toward a model of eye movement control in reading. *Psychological Review*, 105:125–157.

Erik Reichle, Keith Rayner, and Alexander Pollatsek. 2003. The E-Z Reader model of eye-movement control in reading: Comparisons to other models. *Behavioral and Brain Sciences*, 26:445–476.

Erik Reichle, Tessa Warren, and Kerry McConnell. 2009. Using E-Z Reader to model the effects of higher-level language processing on eye movements during reading. *Psychonomic Bulletin & Review*, 16:1–21.

Eric Reichle, editor. 2006a. *Cognitive Systems Research*. 7:1–96. Special issue on models of eye-movement control in reading.

Eric Reichle. 2006b. Computational models of eye movement control in reading: Theories of the "eye-mind" link. *Cognitive Systems Research*, 7:2–3.

Modeling the Noun Phrase versus Sentence Coordination Ambiguity in Dutch: Evidence from Surprisal Theory

Harm Brouwer
University of Groningen
Groningen, the Netherlands
harm.brouwer@rug.nl

Hartmut Fitz
University of Groningen
Groningen, the Netherlands
h.fitz@rug.nl

John C. J. Hoeks
University of Groningen
Groningen, the Netherlands
j.c.j.hoeks@rug.nl

Abstract

This paper investigates whether surprisal theory can account for differential processing difficulty in the NP-/S-coordination ambiguity in Dutch. Surprisal is estimated using a Probabilistic Context-Free Grammar (PCFG), which is induced from an automatically annotated corpus. We find that our lexicalized surprisal model can account for the reading time data from a classic experiment on this ambiguity by Frazier (1987). We argue that syntactic and lexical probabilities, as specified in a PCFG, are sufficient to account for what is commonly referred to as an NP-coordination preference.

1 Introduction

Language comprehension is incremental in that meaning is continuously assigned to utterances as they are encountered word-by-word (Altmann and Kamide, 1999). Not all words, however, are equally easy to process. A word's processing difficulty is affected by, for instance, its frequency or its effect on the syntactic and semantic interpretation of a sentence. A recent theory of sentence processing, surprisal theory (Hale, 2001; Levy, 2008), combines several of these aspects into one single concept, namely the *surprisal* of a word. A word's surprisal is proportional to its expectancy, i.e., the extent to which that word is expected (or predicted). The processing difficulty a word causes during comprehension is argued to be related linearly to its surprisal; the higher the surprisal value of a word, the more difficult it is to process.

In this paper we investigate whether surprisal theory can account for the processing difficulty involved in sentences containing the noun phrase (NP) versus sentence (S) coordination ambiguity. The sentences in (1), from a self-paced reading experiment by Frazier (1987), exemplify this ambiguity:

(1) a. Piet kuste Marie en / **haar zusje** / ook
Piet kissed Marie and / her sister / too
[1,222ms; NP-coordination]

b. Piet kuste Marie en / **haar zusje** / lachte
Piet kissed Marie and / her sister / laughed
[1,596ms; S-coordination]

Both sentences are temporarily ambiguous in the boldface region. Sentence (1-a) is disambiguated as an NP-coordination by the sentence-final adverb ook. Sentence (1-b), on the other hand, is disambiguated as an S-coordination by the sentence-final verb lachte. Frazier found that the verb lachte in sentence (1-b) takes longer to process (1,596 ms) than the adverb ook (1,222 ms) in (1-a).

Frazier (1987) explained these findings by assuming that the human language processor adheres to the so-called *minimal attachment principle*. According to this principle, the sentence processor projects the simplest syntactic structure which is compatible with the material read at any point in time. NP-coordination is syntactically simpler than S-coordination in that it requires less phrasal nodes to be projected. Hence, the processor is biased towards NP- over S-coordination. Processing costs are incurred when this initial preference has to be revised in the disambiguating region, as in sentence (1-b), resulting in longer reading times. Hoeks et al. (2006) have shown that the NP-coordination preference can be reduced, but not entirely eliminated, when poor thematic fit between the verb and a potential object make an NP-coordination less likely (e.g., *Jasper sanded the board and the carpenter laughed*). We argue here that this residual preference for NP-coordination can be explained in terms of syntactic and lexical expectation within the framework of surprisal theory. In contrast to the minimal attachment principle, surprisal theory does not pos-

Proceedings of the 2010 Workshop on Cognitive Modeling and Computational Linguistics, ACL 2010, pages 72–80,
Uppsala, Sweden, 15 July 2010.

tulate specific kinds of syntactic representations or rely on a metric of syntactic complexity to predict processing behavior.

This paper is organized as follows. In section 2 below, we briefly sketch basic surprisal theory. Then we describe how we induced a grammar from a large annotated Dutch corpus and how surprisal was estimated from this grammar (section 3). In section 4, we describe Frazier's experiment on the NP-/S-coordination ambiguity in more detail, and present our surprisal-based simulations of this data. We conclude with a discussion of our results in section 5.

2 Surprisal Theory

As was mentioned in the introduction, language processing is highly incremental, and proceeds on a more or less word-by-word basis. This suggests that a person's difficulty with processing a sentence can be modeled on a word level as proposed by Attneave (1959). Furthermore, it has recently been suggested that one of the characteristics of the comprehension system that makes it so fast, is its ability to anticipate what a speaker will say next. In other words, the language comprehension system works predictively (Otten et al., 2007; van Berkum et al., 2005). Surprisal theory is a model of differential processing difficulty which accommodates both these properties of the comprehension system, incremental processing and word prediction (Hale, 2001; Levy, 2008). In this theory, the processing difficulty of a sentence is a function of word processing difficulty. A word's difficulty is inversely proportional to its expectancy, i.e., the extent to which the word was *expected* or *predicted* in the context in which it occurred. The lower a word's expectancy, the more difficult it is to process. A word's surprisal is linearly related to its difficulty. Consequently, words with lower conditional probabilities (expectancy) lead to higher surprisal than words with higher conditional probabilities.

Surprisal theory is, to some extent, independent of the language model that generates conditional word probabilities. Different models can be used to estimate these probabilities. For all such models, however, a clear distinction can be made between *lexicalized* and *unlexicalized* surprisal. In lexicalized surprisal, the input to the language model is a sequence of words (i.e., a sentence). In unlexicalized surprisal, the input is a sequence of word categories (i.e., part-of-speech tags). While previous studies have used unlexicalized surprisal to predict reading times, evidence for lexicalized surprisal is rather sparse. Smith and Levy (2008) investigated the relation between lexicalized surprisal and reading time data for naturalistic texts. Using a trigram language model, they showed that there was a linear relationship between the two measures. Demberg and Keller (2008) examined whether this relation extended beyond transitional probabilities and found no significant effects. This state of affairs is somewhat unfortunate for surprisal theory since input to the human language processor consists of sequences of words, not part-of-speech tags. In our study we therefore used lexicalized surprisal to investigate whether it can account for reading time data from the NP-/S-coordination ambiguity in Dutch. Lexicalized surprisal furthermore allows us to study how syntactic expectations might be modulated or even reversed by lexical expectations in temporarily ambiguous sentences.

2.1 Probabilistic Context Free Grammars

Both Hale (2001) and Levy (2008) used a Probabilistic Context Free Grammar (PCFG) as a language model in their implementations of surprisal theory. A PCFG consists of a set of rewrite rules which are assigned some probability (Charniak, 1993):

$$\begin{array}{cccc} S & \rightarrow & NP, VP & 1.0 \\ NP & \rightarrow & Det, N & 0.5 \\ NP & \rightarrow & NP, VP & 0.5 \\ \ldots & \rightarrow & \ldots & \ldots \end{array}$$

In this toy grammar, for instance, a noun phrase placeholder can be rewritten to a determiner followed by a noun symbol with probability 0.5. From such a PCFG, the probability of a sentence can be estimated as the product of the probabilities of all the rules used to derive the sentence. If a sentence has multiple derivations, its probability is the sum of the probabilities for each derivation. For our purpose, we also needed to obtain the probability of partial sentences, called *prefix probabilities*. The prefix probability $P(w_1...w_i)$ of a partial sentence $w_1...w_i$ is the sum of the probabilities of all sentences generated by the PCFG which share the initial segment $w_1...w_i$. Hale (2001) pointed out that the ratio of the prefix probabilities $P(w_1 \ldots w_i)$ and $P(w_1 \ldots w_{i-1})$ equals precisely the conditional probability of word w_i. Given a

PCFG, the difficulty of word w_i can therefore be defined as:

$$\text{difficulty}(w_i) \propto -log_2 \left[\frac{P(w_1 \ldots w_i)}{P(w_1 \ldots w_{i-1})} \right].$$

Surprisal theory requires a probabilistic language model that generates some form of word expectancy. The theory itself, however, is largely neutral with respect to which model is employed. Models other than PCFGs can be used to estimate surprisal. Nederhof et al. (1998), for instance, show that prefix probabilities, and therefore surprisal, can be estimated from Tree Adjoining Grammars. This approach was taken in Demberg and Keller (2009). Other approaches have used trigram models (Smith and Levy, 2008), Simple Recurrent Networks of the Elman type (Frank, 2009), Markov models and Echo-state Networks (Frank and Bod, 2010). This illustrates that surprisal theory is not committed to specific claims about the structural representations that language takes in the human mind. It rather functions as a "causal bottleneck" between the representations of a language model, and expectation-based comprehension difficulty (Levy, 2008). In other words, comprehension difficulty does not critically depend on the structural representations postulated by the language model which is harnessed to generate word expectancy.

The use of PCFGs raises some important questions on parallelism in language processing. A prefix probability can be interpreted as a probability distribution over all analyses compatible with a partial sentence. Since partial sentences can sometimes be completed in an indefinite number of ways, it seems both practically and psychologically implausible to implement this distribution as an enumeration over complete structures. Instead, prefix probabilities should be estimated as a by-product of incremental processing, as in Stolcke's (1995) parser (see section 3.2). This approach, however, still leaves open how many analyses are considered in parallel; does the human sentence processor employ full or limited parallelism? Jurafsky (1996) showed that full parallelism becomes more and more unmanageable when the amount of information used for disambiguation increases. Levy, on the other hand, argued that studies of probabilistic parsing reveal that typically a small number of analyses are assigned the majority of probability mass (Roark, 2001). Thus, even when assuming full parallelism, only a small number of 'relevant' analyses would be considered in parallel.

3 Grammar and Parser

3.1 Grammar Induction

In our simulations, we used a PCFG to model the phrase structure of natural language. To induce such a grammar, an annotated corpus was required. We used Alpino (van Noord, 2006)—a robust and wide-coverage dependency parser for Dutch—to automatically generate such a corpus, annotated with phrase structure, for 204.000 sentences, which were randomly extracted from Dutch newspapers. These analyses were then used to induce a PCFG consisting of 650 grammar rules, 89 non-terminals, and 208.133 terminals (lexical items).[1] Moreover, 29 of the 89 non-terminals could result in epsilon productions.

The Alpino parser constructed the phrase structure analyses automatically. Despite Alpino's high accuracy, some analyses might not be entirely correct. Nonetheless, the overall quality of Alpino's analyses is sufficient for corpus studies, and since surprisal theory relies largely on corpus features, we believe the small number of (partially) incorrect analyses should not affect the surprisal estimates computed from our PCFG.

3.2 Earley-Stolcke Parser

To compute prefix probabilities in our model we implemented Stolcke's (1995) probabilistic modification of Earley's (1970) parsing algorithm. An Earley-Stolcke parser is a breadth-first parser. At each point in processing, the parser maintains a collection of *states* that reflect all possible analyses of a partial sentence thus far. A state is a record that keeps track of:

(a) the position up to which a sentence has been processed,

(b) the grammar rule that is applied,

(c) a "dot position" indicating which part of the rule has been processed thus far, and

(d) the leftmost edge of the partial string generated by the rule.

[1] A PCFG can be induced by estimating the relative frequency of each CFG rule $A \rightarrow \alpha$:

$$P(A \rightarrow \alpha) = \frac{count(A \rightarrow \alpha)}{\sum_{\beta} count(A \rightarrow \beta)}.$$

The collection of states is constantly expanded by three operations. First upcoming structural and lexical material is predicted. For all predictions, new states are added with the "dot" placed on the leftmost side of the rule. Then it is determined whether there is a state that predicts the next word in the input sentence. If this is the case, a new state is added with the "dot" placed right to the predicted word. A third operation looks for states with the "dot" rightmost to a grammar rule, and then tries to find states which have the completed state as their leftmost edge. If such states are found, the "dot" in these states is moved to the right of this edge. This step is repeated until no more new states are added. These three operations are cyclically performed until the entire sentence is processed. Our grammar contained 29 non-terminals that could result in epsilon productions. Due to the way epsilon productions are handled within the Earley-Stolcke parser (i.e., by means of "spontaneous dot shifting"), having a large number of epsilon productions leads to a large number of predicted and completed edges. As a consequence, pursuing all possible analyses may become computationally infeasible. To overcome this problem, we modified the Earley-Stolcke parser with a *beam* λ. In prediction and completion, only the λ-number of states with the highest probabilities are added.[2] This constrains the number of states generated by the parser and enforces limited parallelism.

4 NP-/S-coordination ambiguities

4.1 Frazier's experiment

Our aim was to determine to what extent lexicalized surprisal theory can account for reading time data for the NP-/S-coordination ambiguity in Dutch. This type of ambiguity was investigated by Frazier (1987) using a self-paced reading experiment. The sentences in (2) are part of Frazier's materials. Sentence (2-a) and (2-b) exemplify an NP-/S-coordination ambiguity. The sentences are identical and temporarily ambiguous up to the NP haar zusje (her sister). In (2-a) this NP is followed by the adverb ook, and therefore disambiguated to be part of an NP-coordination; Marie and haar zusje are conjoined. In (2-b), on other hand, the same NP is followed by the verb lachte, and therefore disambiguated as the subject of a conjoined sentence; Piet kuste Marie and haar zusje lachte are conjoined.

(2) a. Piet kuste Marie en **haar zusje** ook
Pete kissed Marie and her sister too
(Ambiguous; NP-coordination)

b. Piet kuste Marie en **haar zusje** lachte
Pete kissed Marie and her sister laughed
(Ambiguous; S-coordination)

c. Annie zag **haar zusje** ook
Annie saw her sister too
(Unambiguous; NP-control)

d. Annie zag dat **haar zusje** lachte
Annie saw that her sister laughed
(Unambiguous; S-control)

Sentence (2-c) and (2-d) functioned as unambiguous controls. These sentences are identical up to the verb zag. In (2-c), the verb is followed by the single NP haar zusje, and subsequently the adverb ook. The adverb eliminates the possibility of an NP-coordination. In (2-d), on the other hand, the same verb is followed by the complementizer dat, indicating that the clause her sister laughed is a subordinate clause (the complementizer is obligatory in Dutch).

Frazier constructed twelve sets consisting of four of such sentences each. The 48 sentences were divided into three frames. The first frame included all the material up to the critical NP haar zusje in (2). The second frame contained only the critical NP itself, and the third frame contained all the material that followed this NP.

40 native Dutch speakers participated in the experiment. Reading times for the final frames were collected using a self-paced reading task. Figure 1 depicts the mean reading times for each of the four conditions.

Frazier found a significant interaction between Type of Coordination (NP- versus S-coordination) and Ambiguity (ambiguous versus control) indicating that the effect of disambiguation was larger for S-coordinations (ambiguous: 1596 ms; control: 1141 ms) than for NP-coordinations (ambiguous: 1222 ms; control: 1082 ms).

4.2 Simulations

We simulated Frazier's experiment in our model. Since one set of sentences contained a word that was not covered by our lexicon (set 11; "Lorraine"), we used only eleven of the twelve sets of test items from her study. The remaining 44 sentences were successfully analyzed. In our first

[2] A similar approach was used in Roark (2001) and Frank (2009).

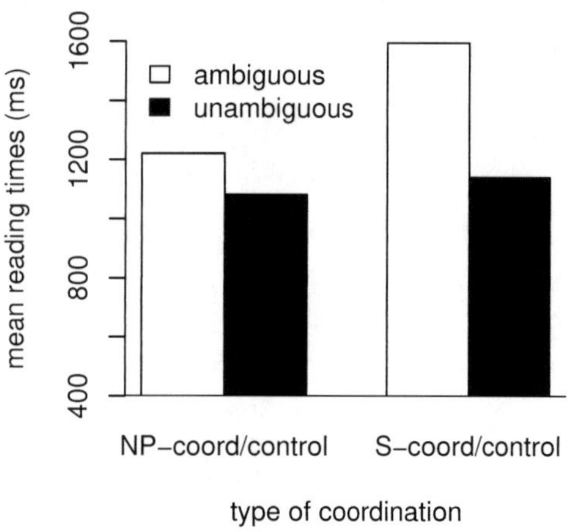

Figure 1: Reading time data for the NP-/S-coordination ambiguity (Frazier, 1987).

simulation we fixed a beam of $\lambda = 16$. Figure 2 depicts surprisal values in the sentence-final frame as estimated by our model. When final frames contained multiple words, we averaged the surprisal values for these words. As Figure 2 shows,

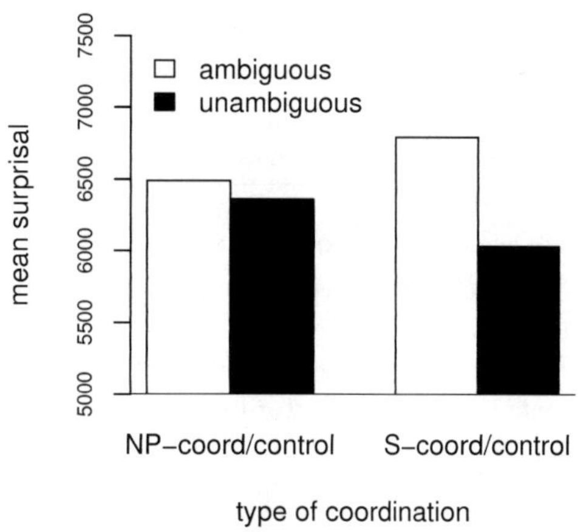

Figure 2: Mean surprisal values for the final frame in the model ($\lambda = 16$).

our model successfully replicated the effects reported in Frazier (1987): In both types of coordinations there was a difference in mean surprisal between the ambiguous sentences and the controls, but in the S-coordinations this effect was larger than in the sentences with NP-coordination. Statistical analyses confirmed our findings. An ANOVA on surprisal values per item revealed an interaction between Type of Coordination (NP- vs. S-coordination) and Ambiguity (ambiguous vs. control), which was marginally significant ($p = 0.06$), most probably due to the small number of

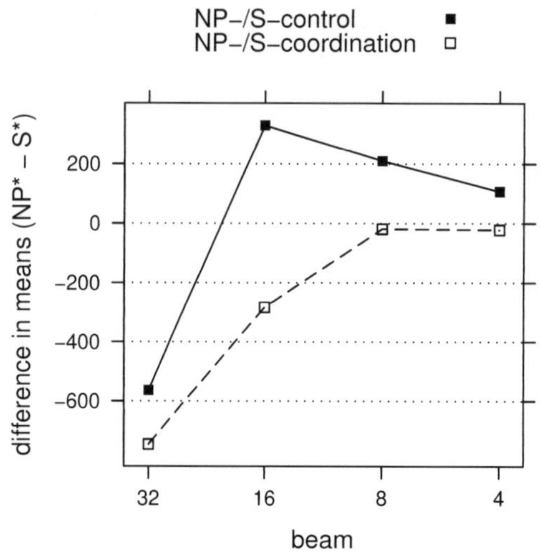

Figure 3: Differences between NP versus S surprisal for different beam sizes (λs).

items (i.e., 11) available for this statistical test (recall that the test in the original experiment was based on 40 participants). Follow-up analyses revealed that the difference between S-coordination and S-control was significant ($p < 0.05$), whereas the difference between NP-coordination and NP-control was not ($p = 0.527$).

To test the robustness of these findings, we repeated the simulation with different beam sizes (λs) by iteratively halving the beam, starting with $\lambda = 32$. Figure 3 shows the differences in mean surprisal between NP-coordination and S-coordination, and NP-control and S-control. With the beam set to four ($\lambda = 4$), we did not obtain full analyses for all test items. Consequently, two sets of items had to be disregarded (sets 8 and 9). For the remaining items, however, we obtained an NP-coordination preference for all beam sizes. The largest difference occurred for $\lambda = 16$. When the beam was set to $\lambda \leq 8$, the difference stabilized. Taking everything into account, the model with $\lambda = 16$ led to the best overall match with Frazier's reading time data.

As for the interaction, Figure 4 depicts the differences in mean surprisal between NP-coordination and NP-control, and S-coordination and S-control. These results indicate that we robustly replicated the interaction between coordination type and ambiguity. For all beam sizes, S-coordination benefited more from disambiguation than NP-coordination, i.e., the difference in means between S-coordination and S-control was larger

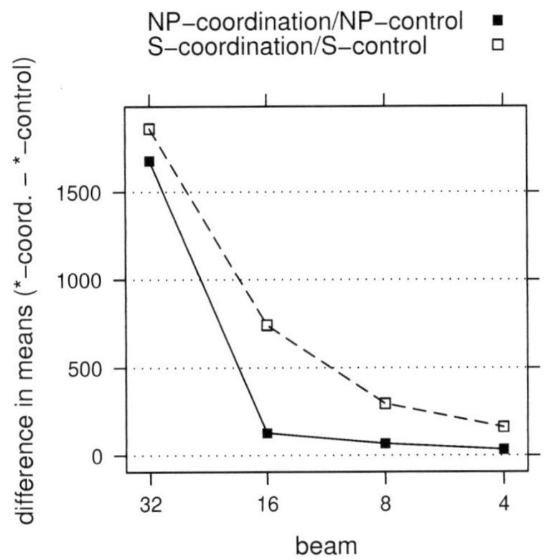

Figure 4: Differences in coordination versus control surprisal for different beam sizes (λs).

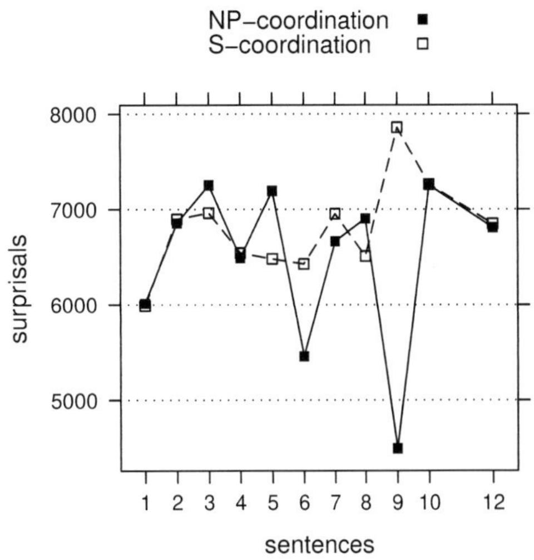

Figure 5: Surprisal per sentence for final frames in the ambiguous condition.

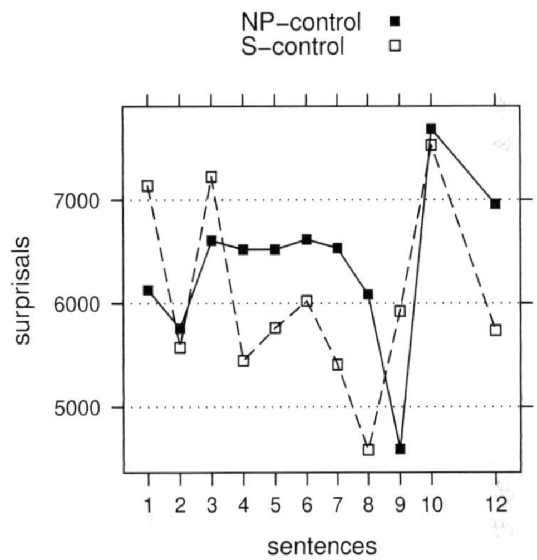

Figure 6: Surprisal per sentence for final frames in the unambiguous condition.

than the difference in means between NP-coordination and NP-control.

In our simulations, we found that surprisal theory can account for reading time data from a classic experiment on the NP-/S-coordination ambiguity in Dutch reported by Frazier (1987). This suggests that the interplay between syntactic and lexical expectancy might be sufficient to explain an NP-coordination preference in human subjects. In the remainder of this section, we analyze our results and explain how this preference arises in the model.

4.3 Model Analysis

To determine what caused the NP-preference in our model, we inspected surprisal differences item-by-item. Whether the NP-coordination preference was syntactic or lexical in nature should be reflected in the grammar. If it was syntactic, NP-coordination would have a higher probability than S-coordination according to our PCFG. If, on the other hand, it was lexical, NP- and S-coordination should be equally probable syntactically. Another possibility, however, is that syntactic and lexical probabilities interacted. If this was the case, we should expect NP-coordinations to lead to lower surprisal values on average only, but not necessarily on every item. Figure 5 shows the estimated surprisal values per sentence-final frame for the ambiguous condition and Figure 6 for the unambiguous condition. Figure 5 indicates that although NP-coordination led to lower surprisal overall (see Figure 2), this was not the case for all tested items. A similar pattern was found for the NP-control versus S-control items in Figure 6. S-controls led to lower surprisal overall, but not for all items. Manual inspection of the grammar revealed a bias towards NP-coordination. A total of 115 PCFG rules concerned coordination ($\approx$ 18% of the entire grammar). As these rules expanded the same grammatical category, their probabilities summed to 1. A rule-by-rule inspection showed that approximately 48% of the probability mass was assigned to rules that dealt with NP-coordinations, 22% to rules that dealt with S-coordinations, and the remaining 30% to rules that dealt with coordination in other structures. In other words, there was a clear preference for NP-coordination in the grammar. Despite this bias, for some tested items the S-coordination received lower surprisal than the NP-coordination (Figure 5). Individual NP-coordination rules might have lower probability than individual S-coordination rules, so the overall preference for NP-coordination in the grammar therefore does not have to be reflected in every test item. Secondly, syntactic probabilities could be modified by lexical probabilities. Suppose for a pair of test items that NP-coordination was syntactically preferred over S-coordination. If the sentence was disambiguated as an NP-coordination by a highly improbable lexical item, and disambiguated as an S-coordination by a highly probable lexical item, surprisal for the NP-coordination might turn out higher than surprisal for the S-coordination. In this way, lexical factors could override the NP-coordination bias in the grammar, leading to a preference for S-coordination in some items.

To summarize, the PCFG displayed an overall NP-coordination preference when surprisal was averaged over the test sentences and this result is consistent with the findings of Frazier (1987). The NP-coordination preference, however, was not invariably reflected on an item-by-item basis. Some S-coordinations showed lower surprisal than the corresponding NP-coordinations. This reversal of processing difficulty can be explained in terms of differences in individual rules, and in terms of interactions between syntactic and lexical probabilities. This suggests that specific lexical expectations might have a much stronger effect on disambiguation preferences than supposed by the minimal attachment principle. Unfortunately, Frazier (1987) only reported mean reading times for the two coordination types.[3] It would be interesting to compare the predictions from our surprisal model with human data item-by-item in order to validate the magnitude of lexical effects we found in the model.

5 Discussion

In this paper we have shown that a model of lexicalized surprisal, based on an automatically induced PCFG, can account for the NP-/S-ambiguity reading time data of Frazier (1987). We found these results to be robust for a critical model parameter (beam size), which suggests that syntactic processing in human comprehension might be based on limited parallelism only. Surprisal theory models processing difficulty on a word level. A word's difficulty is related to the expectations the language processor forms, given the structural and lexical material that precedes it. The model showed a clear preference for NP-coordination which suggests that structural and lexical expectations as estimated from a corpus might be sufficient to explain the NP-coordination bias in human sentence processing.

Our account of this bias differs considerably from the original account proposed by Frazier (minimal attachment principle) in a number of ways. Frazier's explanation is based on a metric of syntactic complexity which in turn depends on quite specific syntactic representations of a language's phrase structure. Surprisal theory, on the other hand, is largely neutral with respect to the form syntactic representations take in the human mind.[4] Moreover, differential processing in surprisal-based models does not require the specification of a notion of syntactic complexity. Both these aspects make surprisal theory a parsimonious explanatory framework. The minimal attachment principle postulates that the bias towards NP-coordination is an initial processing primitive. In contrast, the bias in our simulations is a function of the model's input history and linguistic experience from which the grammar is induced. It is further modulated by the immediate context from which upcoming words are predicted during processing. Consequently, the model's preference for one structural type can vary across sentence tokens and even be reversed on occasion. We argued that our grammar showed an overall preference for NP-coordination but this preference was not necessarily reflected on each and every rule that dealt with coordinations. Some S-coordination rules could have higher probability than NP-coordination rules. In addition, syntactic expectations were modified by lexical expectations. Thus, even when NP-coordination was structurally favored over S-coordination, highly unexpected lexical material could lead to more processing difficulty for NP-coordination than for

[3] Thus it was not possible to determine the strength of the correlation between reading times in Frazier's study and surprisal in our model.

[4] This is not to say, of course, that the choice of language model to estimate surprisal is completely irrelevant; different models will yield different degrees of fit, see Frank and Bod (2010).

S-coordination. Surprisal theory allows us to build a formally precise computational model of reading time data which generates testable, quantitative predictions about the differential processing of individual test items. These predictions (Figure 5) indicate that mean reading times for a set of NP-/S-coordination sentences may not be adequate to tap the origin of differential processing difficulty.

Our results are consistent with the findings of Hoeks et al. (2002), who also found evidence for an NP-coordination preference in a self-paced reading experiment as well as in an eye-tracking experiment. They suggested that NP-coordination might be easier to process because it has a simpler *topic structure* than S-coordination. The former only has one topic, whereas the latter has two. Hoeks et al. (2002) argue that having more than one topic is unexpected. Sentences with more than one topic will therefore cause more processing difficulty. This preference for simple topic-structure that was evident in language comprehension may also be present in language production, and hence in language corpora. Thus, it may very well be the case that the NP-coordination preference that was present in our training corpus may have had a pragmatic origin related to topic-structure. The outcome of our surprisal model is also compatible with the results of Hoeks et al. (2006) who found that thematic information can strongly reduce but not completely eliminate the NP-coordination preference. Surprisal theory is explicitly built on the assumption that multiple sources of information can interact in parallel at any point in time during sentence processing. Accordingly, we suggest here that the residual preference for NP-coordination found in the study of Hoeks et al. (2006) might be explained in terms of syntactic and lexical expectation. And finally, our approach is consistent with a large body of evidence indicating that language comprehension is incremental and makes use of expectation-driven word prediction (Pickering and Garrod, 2007). It remains to be tested whether our model can explain behavioral data from the processing of ambiguities other than the Dutch NP- versus S-coordination case.

References

G. Altmann and Y. Kamide. 1999. Incremental interpretation at verbs: Restricting the domain of subsequent reference. *Cognition*, 73:247–264.

F. Attneave. 1959. *Applications of Information Theory to Psychology: A summary of basic concepts, methods, and results.* Holt, Rinehart and Winston.

E. Charniak. 1993. *Statistical Language Learning.* MIT Press.

V. Demberg and F. Keller. 2008. Data from eye-tracking corpora as evidence for theories of syntactic processing complexity. *Cognition*, 109:193–210.

V. Demberg and F. Keller. 2009. A computational model of prediction in human parsing: Unifying locality and surprisal effects. In *Proceedings of the 31st Annual Conference of the Cognitive Science Society*, Amsterdam, the Netherlands.

J. Earley. 1970. An efficient context-free parsing algorithm. *Communications of the ACM*, 6:451–455.

S. Frank and R. Bod. 2010. The irrelevance of hierarchical structure to human sentence processing. Unpublished manuscript.

S. Frank. 2009. Surprisal-based comparison between a symbolic and a connectionist model of sentence processing. In *Proceedings of the 31th Annual Conference of the Cognitive Science Society*, pages 1139–1144, Amsterdam, the Netherlands.

L. Frazier. 1987. Syntactic processing: Evidence from Dutch. *Natural Langauge and Linguistic Theory*, 5:519–559.

J. Hale. 2001. A probabilistic Earley parser as a psycholinguistic model. In *Proceedings of the 2nd Conference of the North American Chapter of the Association for Computational Linguistics*, volume 2, pages 159–166.

J. Hoeks, W. Vonk, and H. Schriefers. 2002. Processing coordinated structures in context: The effect of topic-structure on ambiguity resolution. *Journal of Memory and Language*, 46:99–119.

J. Hoeks, P. Hendriks, W. Vonk, C. Brown, and P. Hagoort. 2006. Processing the noun phrase versus sentence coordination ambiguity: Thematic information does not completely eliminate processing difficulty. *The Quarterly Journal of Experimental Psychology*, 59:1581–1599.

D. Jurafsky. 1996. A probabilistic model of lexical and syntactic access and disambiguation. *Cognitive Science*, 20:137–147.

R. Levy. 2008. Expectation-based syntactic comprehension. *Cognition*, 106:1126–1177.

M. Nederhof, A. Sarkar, and G. Satta. 1998. Prefix probabilities from stochastic tree adjoining grammar. In *Proceedings of COLING-ACL '98*, pages 953–959, Montreal.

M. Otten, M. Nieuwland, and J. van Berkum. 2007. Great expectations: Specific lexical anticipation influences the processing of spoken language. *BMC Neuroscience*.

M. Pickering and S. Garrod. 2007. Do people use language production to make predictions during comprehension? *Trends in Cognitive Sciences*, 11:105–110.

B. Roark. 2001. Probabilistic top-down parsing and language modeling. *Computational Linguistics*, 27:249–276.

N. Smith and R. Levy. 2008. Optimal processing times in reading: A formal model and empirical investigation. In *Proceedings of the 30th annual conference of the Cognitive Science Society*, pages 595–600, Austin, TX.

A. Stolcke. 1995. An efficient probabilistic context-free parsing algorithm that computes prefix probabilities. *Computational linguistics*, 21:165–201.

J. van Berkum, C. Brown, P. Zwitserlood, V. Kooijman, and P. Hagoort. 2005. Anticipating upcoming words in discourse: Evidence from ERPs and reading times. *Journal of Experimental Psychology: Learning, Memory, and Cognition*, 31:443–467.

G. van Noord. 2006. At last parsing is now operational. In *Verbum Ex Machina. Actes de la 13e conférence sur le traitement automatique des langues naturelles*, pages 20–42. Presses universitaires de Louvain.

Uncertainty reduction as a measure of cognitive processing effort

Stefan L. Frank
University of Amsterdam
Amsterdam, The Netherlands
s.l.frank@uva.nl

Abstract

The amount of cognitive effort required to process a word has been argued to depend on the word's effect on the uncertainty about the incoming sentence, as quantified by the entropy over sentence probabilities. The current paper tests this hypothesis more thoroughly than has been done before by using recurrent neural networks for entropy-reduction estimation. A comparison between these estimates and word-reading times shows that entropy reduction is positively related to processing effort, confirming the entropy-reduction hypothesis. This effect is independent from the effect of surprisal.

1 Introduction

In the field of computational psycholinguistics, a currently popular approach is to account for reading times on a sentence's words by estimates of the amount of information conveyed by these words. Processing a word that conveys more information is assumed to involve more cognitive effort, which is reflected in the time required to read the word.

In this context, the most common formalization of a word's information content is its surprisal (Hale, 2001; Levy, 2008). If word string w_1^t (short for $w_1, w_2, \ldots w_t$) is the sentence so far and $P(w_{t+1}|w_1^t)$ the occurrence probability of the next word w_{t+1}, then that word's surprisal is defined as $-\log P(w_{t+1}|w_1^t)$. It is well established by now that word-reading times indeed correlate positively with surprisal values as estimated by any sufficiently accurate generative language model (Boston et al., 2008; Demberg and Keller, 2008; Frank, 2009; Roark et al., 2009; Smith and Levy, 2008).

A lesser known alternative operationalization of a word's information content is based on the uncertainty about the rest of the sentence, quantified by Hale (2003, 2006) as the entropy of the probability distribution over possible sentence structures. The reduction in entropy that results from processing a word is taken to be the amount of information conveyed by that word, and was argued by Hale to be predictive of word-reading time. However, this entropy-reduction hypothesis has not yet been comprehensively tested, possibly because of the difficulty of computing the required entropies. Although Hale (2006) shows how sentence entropy can be computed given a PCFG, this computation is not feasible when the grammar is of realistic size.

Here, we empirically investigate the entropy-reduction hypothesis more thoroughly than has been done before, by using recurrent neural networks as language models. Since these networks do not derive any structure, they provide estimates of *sentence* entropy rather than sentence-*structure* entropy. In practice, these two entropies will generally be similar: If the rest of the sentence is highly uncertain, so is its structure. Sentence entropy can therefore be viewed as a simplification of structure entropy; one that is less theory dependent since it does not rely on any particular grammar. The distinction between entropy over sentences and entropy over structures will simply be ignored in the remainder of this paper.

Results show that, indeed, a significant fraction of variance in reading-time data is accounted for by entropy reduction, over and above surprisal.

2 Entropy and sentence processing

2.1 Sentence entropy

Let W be the set of words in the language and W^i the set of all word strings of length i. The set of complete sentences, denoted $\mathcal{S}$, contains all word strings of any length (i.e., $\bigcup_{i=0}^{\infty} W^i$), except that a special end-of-sentence marker </s> is attached to the end of each string.

Proceedings of the 2010 Workshop on Cognitive Modeling and Computational Linguistics, ACL 2010, pages 81–89,
Uppsala, Sweden, 15 July 2010.

A generative language model defines a probability distribution over $\mathcal{S}$. The entropy of this distribution is

$$H = -\sum_{w_1^j \in \mathcal{S}} P(w_1^j) \log P(w_1^j).$$

As words are processed one by one, the sentence probabilities change. When the first t words (i.e., the string $w_1^t \in W^t$) of a sentence have been processed, the entropy of the probability distribution over sentences is

$$H(t) = -\sum_{w_1^j \in \mathcal{S}} P(w_1^j | w_1^t) \log P(w_1^j | w_1^t). \quad (1)$$

In order to simplify later equations, we define the function $h(y|x) = -P(y|x) \log P(y|x)$, such that Eq. 1 becomes

$$H(t) = \sum_{w_1^j \in \mathcal{S}} h(w_1^j | w_1^t).$$

If the first t words of w_1^j do not equal w_1^t (or w_1^j has fewer than $t+1$ words),[1] then $P(w_1^j | w_1^t) = 0$ so $h(w_1^j | w_1^t) = 0$. This means that, for computing $H(t)$, only the words from $t+1$ onwards need to be taken into account:

$$H(t) = \sum_{w_{t+1}^j \in \mathcal{S}} h(w_{t+1}^j | w_1^t).$$

The reduction in entropy due to processing the next word, w_{t+1}, is

$$\Delta H(t+1) = H(t) - H(t+1). \quad (2)$$

Note that positive ΔH corresponds to a *decrease* in entropy. According to Hale (2006), the nonnegative reduction in entropy (i.e., $\max\{0, \Delta H\}$) reflects the cognitive effort involved in processing w_{t+1} and should therefore be predictive of reading time on that word.

2.2 Suffix entropy

Computing $H(t)$ is computationally feasible only when there are very few sentences in $\mathcal{S}$, or when the language can be described by a small grammar. To estimate entropy in more realistic situations, an obvious solution is to look only at the next few words instead of all complete continuations of w_1^t.

Let $\mathcal{S}^m$ be the subset of $\mathcal{S}$ containing all (and only) sentences of length m or less, counting also the </s> at the end of each sentence. Note that this set includes the 'empty sentence' consisting of only </s>. The set of length-m word strings that do not end in </s> is W^m. Together, these sets form $\mathcal{W}^m = W^m \cup \mathcal{S}^m$, which contains all the relevant strings for defining the entropy over strings up to length m.[2] After processing w_1^t, the entropy over strings up to length $t+n$ is:

$$H_n(t) = \sum_{w_1^j \in \mathcal{W}^{t+n}} h(w_1^j | w_1^t) = \sum_{w_{t+1}^j \in \mathcal{W}^n} h(w_{t+1}^j | w_1^t).$$

It now seems straightforward to define suffix-entropy reduction by analogy with sentence-entropy reduction as expressed in Eq. 2: Simply replace H by H_n to obtain

$$\Delta H_n^{\text{suf}}(t+1) = H_n(t) - H_n(t+1). \quad (3)$$

As indicated by its superscript label, ΔH_n^{suf} quantifies the reduction in uncertainty about the upcoming n-word suffix. However, this is conceptually different from the original ΔH of Eq. 2, which is the reduction in uncertainty about the identity of the current sentence. The difference becomes clear when we view the sentence processor's task as that of selecting the correct element from $\mathcal{S}$. If this set of complete sentences is approximated by $\mathcal{W}^{t+n}$, and the task is to select one element from that set, an alternative definition of suffix-entropy reduction arises:

$$\begin{aligned} &\Delta H_n^{\text{sent}}(t+1) \\ &= \sum_{w_1^j \in \mathcal{W}^{t+n}} h(w_1^j | w_1^t) - \sum_{w_1^j \in \mathcal{W}^{t+n}} h(w_1^j | w_1^{t+1}) \\ &= \sum_{w_{t+1}^j \in \mathcal{W}^n} h(w_{t+1}^j | w_1^t) - \sum_{w_{t+2}^j \in \mathcal{W}^{n-1}} h(w_{t+2}^j | w_1^{t+1}) \\ &= H_n(t) - H_{n-1}(t+1). \quad (4) \end{aligned}$$

The label 'sent' indicates that ΔH_n^{sent} quantifies the reduction in uncertainty about which sentence forms the current input. This uncertainty is approximated by marginalizing over all word strings longer than $t+n$.

It is easy to see that

$$\lim_{n\to\infty} \Delta H_n^{\text{suf}} = \lim_{n\to\infty} \Delta H_n^{\text{sent}} = \Delta H,$$

[1] Since w_1^j ends with </s> and w_1^t does not, the two strings must be different. Consequently, if w_1^j is t words long, then $P(w_1^j | w_1^t) = 0$.

[2] The probability of a string $w_1^m \in W^m$ is the summed probability of all sentences with prefix w_1^m.

so both approximations of entropy reduction appropriately converge to ΔH in the limit. Nevertheless, they formalize different quantities and may well correspond to different cognitive factors. If it is true that cognitive effort is predicted by the reduction in uncertainty about the identity of the incoming sentence, we should find that word-reading times are predicted more accurately by ΔH_n^{sent} than by ΔH_n^{suf}.

2.3 Relation to next-word entropy

In the extreme case of $n = 1$, Eq. 4 reduces to

$$\Delta H_1^{\text{sent}}(t+1) = H_1(t) - H_0(t+1) = H_1(t),$$

so the reduction of entropy over the single next word w_{t+1} equals the next-word entropy just before processing that word. Note that $\Delta H_1^{\text{sent}}(t+1)$ is independent of the word at $t+1$, making it a severely impoverished measure of the uncertainty reduction caused by that word. We would therefore expect reading times to be predicted more accurately by ΔH_n^{sent} with $n > 1$, and possibly even by ΔH_1^{suf}.

Roark et al. (2009) investigated the relation between $H_1(t+1)$ and reading time on w_{t+1}, and found a significant positive effect: Larger next-word entropy directly *after* processing w_{t+1} corresponded to longer reading time *on* that word. This is of particular interest because $H_1(t+1)$ necessarily correlates *negatively* with entropy reduction $\Delta H_n^{\text{sent}}(t+1)$: If entropy is large after w_{t+1}, chances are that it did not reduce much through processing of w_{t+1}. Indeed, in our data set, $H_1(t+1)$ and $\Delta H_n^{\text{sent}}(t+1)$ correlate between $r = -.29$ and $r = -.26$ (for $n = 2$ to $n = 4$) which is highly significantly ($p \approx 0$) different from 0. Roark et al.'s finding of a positive relation between $H_1(t+1)$ and reading time on w_{t+1} therefore seems to disconfirm the entropy-reduction hypothesis.

3 Method

A set of language models was trained on a corpus of POS tags of sentences. The advantage of using POS tags rather than words is that their probabilities can be estimated much more accurately and, consequently, more accurate prediction of word-reading time is possible (Demberg and Keller, 2008; Roark et al., 2009). Subsequent to training, the models were made to generate estimates of surprisal and entropy reductions ΔH_n^{suf} and ΔH_n^{sent} over a test corpus. These estimates were then compared to reading times measured over the words of the same test corpus. This section presents the data sets that were used, language-model details, and the evaluation metric.

3.1 Data

The models were trained on the POS tag sequences of the full WSJ corpus (Marcus et al., 1993). They were evaluated on the POS-tagged Dundee corpus (Kennedy and Pynte, 2005), which has been used in several studies that investigate the relation between word surprisal and reading time (Demberg and Keller, 2008; Frank, 2009; Smith and Levy, 2008). This 2 368-sentence (51 501 words) collection of British newspaper editorials comes with eye-tracking data of 10 participants. POS tags for the Dundee corpus were taken from Frank (2009).

For each word and each participant, reading time was defined as the total fixation time on that word before any fixation on a later word of the same sentence. Following Demberg and Keller (2008), data points (i.e., word/participant pairs) were removed if the word was not fixated, was presented as the first or last on a line, contained more than one capital letter or a non-letter (e.g., the apostrophe in a clitic), or was attached to punctuation. Mainly due to the large number (over 46%) of nonfixations, 62.8% of data points were removed, leaving 191 380 data points (between 16 469 and 21 770 per participant).

3.2 Language model

Entropy is more time consuming to compute than surprisal, even for $n = 1$, because it requires estimates of the occurrence probabilities at $t+1$ of *all* word types, rather than just of the actual next word. Moreover, the number of suffixes rises exponentially as suffix length n grows, and, consequently, so does computation time.

Roark et al. (2009) used an incremental PCFG parser to obtain H_1 but this method rapidly becomes infeasible as n grows. Low-order Markov models (e.g., a bigram model) are more efficient and can be used for larger n but they do not form particularly accurate language models. Moreover, Markov models lack cognitive plausibility.

Here, Simple Recurrent Networks (SRNs) (Elman, 1990) are used as language models. When trained to predict the upcoming input in a word sequence, these networks can generate estimates of

$P(w_{t+1}|w_1^t)$ efficiently and relatively accurately. They thereby allow to approximate sentence entropy more closely than the incremental parsers used in previous studies. Unlike Markov models, SRNs have been claimed to form cognitively realistic sentence-processing models (Christiansen and MacDonald, 2009). Moreover, it has been shown that SRN-based surprisal estimates can correlate more strongly to reading times than surprisal values estimated by a phrase-structure grammar (Frank, 2009).

3.2.1 Network architecture and processing

The SRNs comprised three layers of units: the input layer, the recurrent (hidden) layer, and the output layer. Each input unit corresponds to one POS tag, making 45 input units since there are 45 different POS tags in the WSJ corpus. The network's output units represent predictions of subsequent inputs. The output layer also has one unit for each POS tag, plus an extra unit that represents </s>, that is, the absence of any further input. Hence, there were 46 output units. The number of recurrent units was fairly arbitrarily set to 100.

As is common in these networks, the input layer was fully connected to the recurrent layer, which in turn was fully connected to the output layer. Also, there were time-delayed connections from the recurrent layer to itself. In addition, each recurrent and output unit received a bias input.

The vectors of recurrent- and output-layer activations after processing w_1^t are denoted $\mathbf{a}_{\text{rec}}(t)$ and $\mathbf{a}_{\text{out}}(t)$, respectively. At the beginning of each sentence, $\mathbf{a}_{\text{rec}}(0) = 0.5$.

The input vector $\mathbf{a}_{\text{in}}^i$, representing POS tag i, consists of zeros except for a single element (corresponding to i) that equals one. When input i is processed, the recurrent layer's state is updated according to:

$$\mathbf{a}_{\text{rec}}(t) = \mathbf{f}_{\text{rec}}(\mathbf{W}_{\text{rec}}\mathbf{a}_{\text{rec}}(t-1) + \mathbf{W}_{\text{in}}\mathbf{a}_{\text{in}}^i + \mathbf{b}_{\text{rec}}),$$

where matrices $\mathbf{W}_{\text{in}}$ and $\mathbf{W}_{\text{rec}}$ contain the network's input and recurrent connection weights, respectively; $\mathbf{b}_{\text{rec}}$ is the vector of recurrent-layer biases; and activation function $\mathbf{f}_{\text{rec}}(\mathbf{x})$ is the logistic function $f(x) = (1+\mathrm{e}^{-x})^{-1}$ applied elementwise to $\mathbf{x}$. The new output vector is now given by

$$\mathbf{a}_{\text{out}}(t) = \mathbf{f}_{\text{out}}(\mathbf{W}_{\text{out}}\mathbf{a}_{\text{rec}}(t) + \mathbf{b}_{\text{out}}),$$

where $\mathbf{W}_{\text{out}}$ is the matrix of output connection weights; $\mathbf{b}_{\text{out}}$ the vector of output-layer biases; and $\mathbf{f}_{\text{out}}(\mathbf{x})$ the softmax function

$$f_{i,\text{out}}(x_1, \ldots, x_{46}) = \frac{\mathrm{e}^{x_i}}{\sum_j \mathrm{e}^{x_j}}.$$

This function makes sure that $\mathbf{a}_{\text{out}}$ sums to one and can therefore be viewed as a probability distribution: The i-th element of $\mathbf{a}_{\text{out}}(t)$ is the SRN's estimate of the probability that the i-th POS tag will be the input at $t+1$, or, in case i corresponds to </s>, the probability that the sentence ends after t POS tags.

3.2.2 Network training

Ten SRNs, differing only in their random initial connection weights and biases, were trained using the standard backpropagation algorithm. Each string of WSJ POS tags was presented once, with the sentences in random order. After each POS input, connection weights were updated to minimize the cross-entropy between the network outputs and a 46-element vector that encoded the next input (or marked the end of the sentence) by the corresponding element having a value of one and all others being zero.

3.3 Evaluation

3.3.1 Obtaining surprisal and entropy

Since $\mathbf{a}_{\text{out}}(t)$ is basically the probability distribution $P(w_{t+1}|w_1^t)$, surprisal and H_1 can be read off directly. To obtain H_2, H_3, and H_4, we use the fact that

$$P(w_{t+1}^{t+n}|w_1^t) = \prod_{i=1}^{n} P(w_{t+i}|w_1^{t+i-1}). \quad (5)$$

Surprisal and entropy estimates were averaged over the ten SRNs. So, for each POS tag of the Dundee corpus, there was one estimate of surprisal and four of entropy (for $n = 1$ to $n = 4$).

Since $H_n(t)$ approximates $H(t)$ more closely as n grows, it would be natural to expect a better fit to reading times for larger n. On the other hand, it goes without saying that H_n is only a very rough measure of a reader's actual uncertainty about the upcoming n inputs, no matter how accurate the language model that was used to compute these entropies. Crucially, the correspondence between H_n and the uncertainty experienced by a reader will grow even weaker with larger n. This is apparent from the fact that, as proven in the Appendix, H_n can be expressed in terms of H_1 and H_{n-1}:

$$H_n(t) = H_1(t) + E(H_{n-1}(t+1)),$$

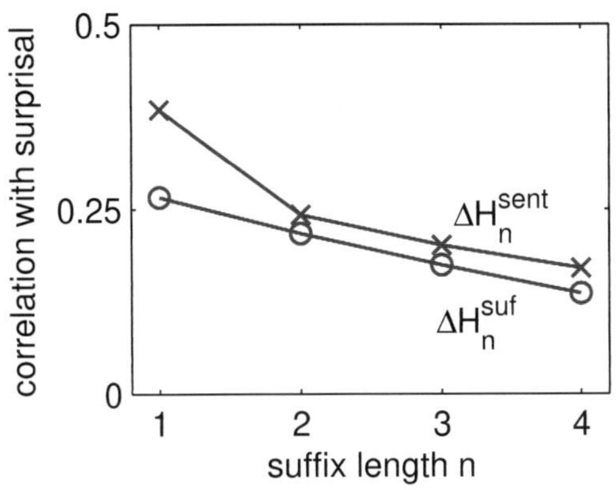

Figure 1: Coefficient of correlation between estimates of surprisal and entropy reduction, as a function of suffix length n.

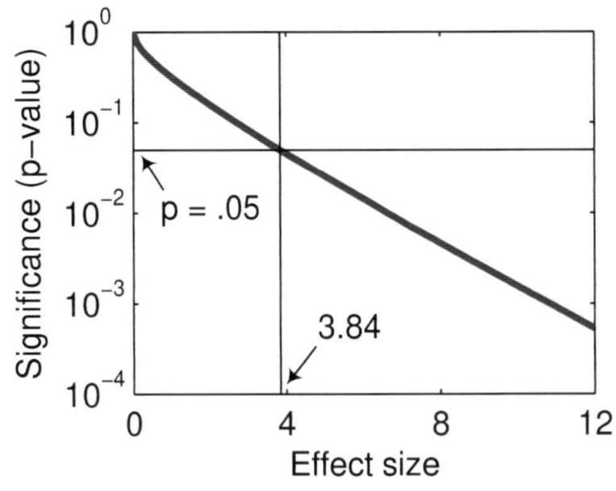

Figure 2: Cumulative χ^2 distribution with 1 degree of freedom, plotting statistical significance (p-value) as a function of effect size.

where $E(x)$ is the expected value of x. Obviously, the expected value of H_{n-1} is less appropriate as an uncertainty measure than is H_{n-1} itself. Hence, H_n can be less accurate than H_{n-1} as a quantification of the actual cognitive uncertainty. For this reason, we may expect larger n to result in *worse* fit to reading-time data.[3]

3.3.2 Negative entropy reduction

Hale (2006) argued for nonnegative entropy reduction $\max\{0, \Delta H\}$, rather than ΔH itself, as a measure of processing effort. For ΔH^{sent}, the difference between the two is negligible because only about 0.03% of entropy reductions are negative. As for ΔH^{suf}, approximately 42% of values are negative so whether these are left out makes quite a difference. Since preliminary experiments showed that word-reading times are predicted much more accurately by ΔH^{suf} than by $\max\{0, \Delta H^{\text{suf}}\}$, only ΔH^{suf} and ΔH^{sent} were used here, that is, negative values were included.

3.3.3 Relation between information measures

Both surprisal and entropy reduction can be taken as measures for the amount of information conveyed by a word, so it is to be expected that they are positively correlated. However, as shown in Figure 1, this correlation is in fact quite weak, ranging from .14 for ΔH^{suf}_4 to .38 for ΔH^{sent}_1. In contrast, ΔH^{suf}_n and ΔH^{sent}_n correlate very strongly to each other: The coefficients of correlation range from .73 when $n = 1$ to .97 for $n = 4$.

[3]Not to mention the realistic possibility that the cognitive sentence-processing system does not abide by the normative chain rule expressed in Eq. 5.

3.3.4 Fit to reading times

A generalized linear regression model for gamma-distributed data was fitted to the reading times.[4] This model contained several well-known predictors of word-reading time: the number of letters in the word, the word's position in the sentence, whether the next word was fixated, whether the previous word was fixated, log of the word's relative frequency, log of the word's forward and backward transitional probabilities,[5] and surprisal of the part-of-speech. Next, one set of entropy-reduction estimates was added to the regression. The *effect size* is the resulting decrease in the regression model's deviance, which is indicative of the amount of variance in reading time accounted for by those estimates of entropy reduction. Figure 2 shows how effect size is related to statistical significance: A factor forms a significant ($p < .05$) predictor of reading time if its effect size is greater than 3.84.

4 Results and Discussion

4.1 Effect of entropy reduction

Figure 3 shows the effect sizes for both measures of entropy reduction, and their relation to suffix length n. All effects are in the correct direction, that is, larger entropy reduction corresponds to longer reading time. These results clearly support the entropy-reduction hypothesis: A significant

[4]The reading times, which are approximately gamma distributed, were first normalized to make the scale parameters of the gamma distributions the same across participants.

[5]These are, respectively, the relative frequency of the word given the previous word, and its relative frequency given the next word.

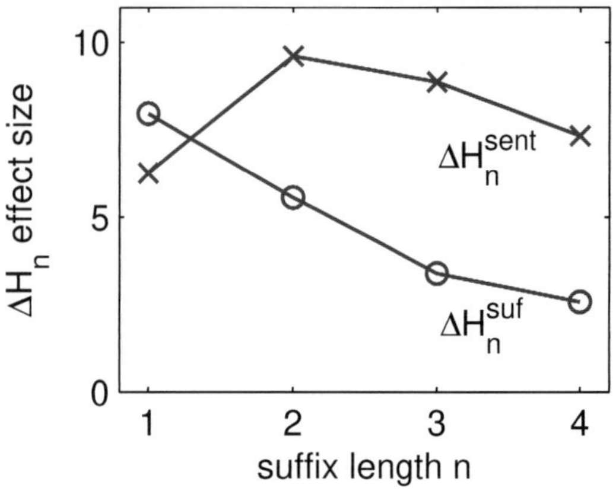

Figure 3: Size of the effect of ΔH_n^{suf} and ΔH_n^{sent} as a function of suffix length n.

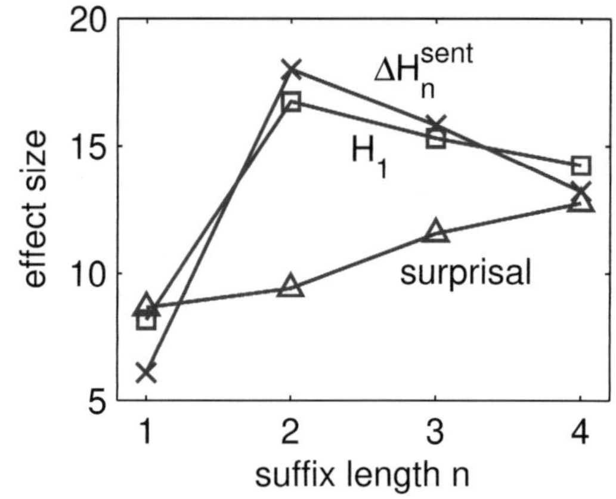

Figure 4: Effect size of entropy reduction (ΔH_n^{sent}), next-word entropy (H_1), or surprisal, over and above the other two predictors.

fraction of variance in reading time is accounted for by the entropy-reduction estimates ΔH_n^{sent}, over and above what is explained by the other factors in the regression analysis, including surprisal. Moreover, the effect of ΔH_n^{sent} is larger than that of ΔH_n^{suf}, indicating that it is indeed uncertainty about the identity of the current sentence, rather than uncertainty about the upcoming input(s), that matters for cognitive processing effort. Only at $n = 1$ was the effect size of ΔH_n^{sent} smaller than that of ΔH_n^{suf}, but it should be kept in mind that ΔH_1^{sent} is independent of the incoming word and is therefore quite impoverished as a measure of the effort involved in processing the word. Moreover, the difference between ΔH_1^{sent} and ΔH_1^{suf} is not significant ($p > .4$), as determined by the bootstrap method (Efron and Tibshirani, 1986). In contrast, the differences are significant when $n > 1$ (all $p < .01$), in spite of the high correlation between ΔH_n^{sent} and ΔH_n^{suf}.

Another indication that cognitive processing effort is modeled more accurately by ΔH_n^{sent} than by ΔH_n^{suf} is that the effect size of ΔH_n^{sent} seems less affected by n. Even though ΔH, the reduction in entropy over complete sentences, is approximated more closely as suffix length grows, increasing n is strongly detrimental to the effect of ΔH_n^{suf}: It is no longer significant for $n > 2$. Presumably, this can be (partly) attributed to the impoverished relation between formal entropy and psychological uncertainty, as explained in Section 3.3.1. In any case, the effect of ΔH_n^{sent} is more stable. Although ΔH_n^{suf} and ΔH_n^{sent} necessarily converge as $n \to \infty$, the two effect sizes seem to diverge up to $n = 3$: The difference between the effect sizes of ΔH_n^{sent} and ΔH_n^{suf} is marginally significantly ($p < .07$) larger for $n = 3$ than for $n = 2$.

4.2 Effects of other factors

It is also of interest that surprisal has a significant effect over and above entropy reduction, in the correct (i.e., positive) direction. When surprisal estimates are added to a regression model that already contains ΔH_n^{sent}, the effect size ranges from 8.7 for $n = 1$ to 13.9 for $n = 4$. This show that there exist independent effects of surprisal and entropy reduction on processing effort.

Be reminded from Section 2.3 that Roark et al. (2009) found a positive relation between reading time on w_{t+1} and $H_1(t+1)$, the next-word entropy after processing w_{t+1}. When that value is added as a predictor in the regression model that already contains surprisal and entropy reduction ΔH_n^{sent}, model fit greatly improves. In fact, as can be seen from comparing Figures 3 and 4, the effect of ΔH_n^{sent} is strengthened by including next-word entropy in the regression model. Moreover, each of the factors surprisal, entropy reduction, and next-word entropy has a significant effect over and above the other two. In all cases, these effects were in the positive direction. This confirms Roark et al.'s finding and shows that it is in fact compatible with the entropy-reduction hypothesis, in contrast to what was suggested in Section 2.3.

5 Discussion and conclusion

The current results contribute to a growing body of evidence that the amount of information conveyed by a word in sentence context is indicative of the amount of cognitive effort required for processing, as can be observed from reading time on the word. Several previous studies have shown that surprisal can serve as a cognitively relevant measure for a word's information content. In contrast, the relevance of entropy reduction as a cognitive measure has not been investigated this thoroughly before. Hale (2003; 2006) presents entropy-reduction accounts of particular psycholinguistic phenomena, but does not show that entropy reduction generally correlates with word-reading times. Roark et al. (2009) presented data that could be taken as evidence against the entropy-reduction hypothesis, but the current paper showed that the next-word entropy effect, found by Roark et al., is independent of the entropy-reduction effect.

It is tempting to take the independent effects of surprisal and entropy reduction as evidence for two distinct cognitive representations or processes, one related to surprisal, the other to entropy reduction. However, it is very well possible that these two information measures are merely complementary formalizations of a single, cognitively relevant notion of word information. Since the quantitative results presented here provide no evidence for either view, a more detailed qualitative analysis is needed.

In addition, the relation between reading time and the two measures of word information may be further clarified by the development of mechanistic sentence-processing models. Both the surprisal and entropy-reduction theories provide only functional-level descriptions (Marr, 1982) of the relation between information content and processing effort, so the question remains which underlying mechanism is responsible for longer reading times on words that convey more information. That is, we are still without a model that proposes, at Marr's computational level, some specific sentence-processing mechanism that takes longer to process a word that has higher surprisal or leads to greater reduction in sentence entropy. For surprisal, Levy (2008) makes a first step in that direction by presenting a mechanistic account of why surprisal would predict word-reading time: If the state of the sentence-processing system is viewed as a probability distribution over all possible interpretations of complete sentences, and processing a word comes down to updating this distribution to incorporate the new information, then the word's surprisal equals the Kullback-Leibler divergence from the old distribution to the new. This divergence is presumed to quantify the amount of work (and, therefore, time) needed to update the distribution. Likewise, Smith and Levy (2008) explain the surprisal effect in terms of a reader's optimal preparation to incoming input. When it comes to entropy reduction, however, no reading-time predicting mechanism has been proposed. Ideally, of course, there should be a single computational-level model that predicts the effects of both surprisal and entropy reduction.

One recent model (Frank, 2010) shows that the reading-time effects of both surprisal and entropy reduction can indeed result from a single processing mechanism. The model simulates sentence comprehension as the incremental and dynamical update of a non-linguistic representation of the state-of-affairs described by the sentence. In this framework, surprisal and entropy reduction are defined with respect to a probabilistic model of the *world*, rather than a model of the *language*: The amount of information conveyed by a word depends on what is asserted by the sentence-so-far, and not on how the sentence's form matches the statistical patterns of the language. As it turns out, word-processing times in the sentence-comprehension model correlate positively with both surprisal and entropy reduction. The model thereby forms a computational-level account of the relation between reading time and both measures of word information. According to this account, the two information measures do not correspond to two distinct cognitive processes. Rather, there is one comprehension mechanism that is responsible for the incremental revision of a mental representation. Surprisal and entropy reduction form two complementary quantifications of the extent of this revision.

Acknowledgments

The research presented here was supported by grant 277-70-006 of the Netherlands Organization for Scientific Research (NWO). I would like to thank Rens Bod, Reut Tsarfaty, and two anonymous reviewers for their helpful comments.

References

M. F. Boston, J. Hale, U. Patil, R. Kliegl, and S. Vasishth. 2008. Parsing costs as predictors of reading difficulty: An evaluation using the Potsdam Sentence Corpus. *Journal of Eye Movement Research*, 2:1–12.

M. H. Christiansen and M. C. MacDonald. 2009. A usage-based approach to recursion in sentence processing. *Language Learning*, 59:129–164.

V. Demberg and F. Keller. 2008. Data from eye-tracking corpora as evidence for theories of syntactic processing complexity. *Cognition*, 109:193–210.

B. Efron and R. Tibshirani. 1986. Bootstrap methods for standard errors, confidence intervals, and other measures of statistical accuracy. *Statistical Science*, 1:54–75.

J. L. Elman. 1990. Finding structure in time. *Cognitive Science*, 14:179–211.

S. L. Frank. 2009. Surprisal-based comparison between a symbolic and a connectionist model of sentence processing. In N. A. Taatgen and H. van Rijn, editors, *Proceedings of the 31st Annual Conference of the Cognitive Science Society*, pages 1139–1144. Austin, TX: Cognitive Science Society.

S. L. Frank. 2010. The role of world knowledge in sentence comprehension: an information-theoretic analysis and a connectionist simulation. *Manuscript in preparation.*

J. Hale. 2001. A probabilistic Early parser as a psycholinguistic model. In *Proceedings of the second conference of the North American chapter of the Association for Computational Linguistics*, volume 2, pages 159–166. Pittsburgh, PA: Association for Computational Linguistics.

J. Hale. 2003. The information conveyed by words. *Journal of Psycholinguistic Research*, 32:101–123.

J. Hale. 2006. Uncertainty about the rest of the sentence. *Cognitive Science*, 30:643–672.

A. Kennedy and J. Pynte. 2005. Parafoveal-on-foveal effects in normal reading. *Vision Research*, 45:153–168.

R. Levy. 2008. Expectation-based syntactic comprehension. *Cognition*, 106:1126–1177.

M. Marcus, B. Santorini, and M. A. Marcinkiewicz. 1993. Building a large annotated corpus of english: the Penn Treebank. *Computational Linguistics*, 19:313–330.

D. Marr. 1982. *Vision*. San Francisco: W.H. Freeman and Company.

B. Roark, A. Bachrach, C. Cardenas, and C. Pallier. 2009. Deriving lexical and syntactic expectation-based measures for psycholinguistic modeling via incremental top-down parsing. In *Proceedings of the 2009 Conference on Empirical Methods in Natural Language Processing*, pages 324–333. Association for Computational Linguistics.

N. J. Smith and R. Levy. 2008. Optimal processing times in reading: a formal model and empirical investigation. In B. C. Love, K. McRae, and V. M. Sloutsky, editors, *Proceedings of the 30th Annual Conference of the Cognitive Science Society*, pages 595–600. Austin, TX: Cognitive Science Society.

Appendix

It is of some interest that H_n can be expressed in terms of H_1 and the expected value of H_{n-1}. First, note that

$$\begin{aligned} h(w_{t+1}^j|w_1^t) &= -P(w_{t+1}^j|w_1^t)\log P(w_{t+1}^j|w_1^t) \\ &= -P(w_{t+1}|w_1^t)P(w_{t+2}^j|w_1^{t+1})\log\left(P(w_{t+1}|w_1^t)P(w_{t+2}^j|w_1^{t+1})\right) \\ &= P(w_{t+2}^j|w_1^{t+1})h(w_{t+1}|w_1^t) + P(w_{t+1}|w_1^t)h(w_{t+2}^j|w_1^{t+1}). \end{aligned}$$

For entropy $H_n(t)$, this makes

$$\begin{aligned} H_n(t) &= \sum_{w_{t+1}^j\in\mathcal{W}^n} h(w_{t+1}^j|w_1^t) \\ &= \sum_{w_{t+1}^j\in\mathcal{W}^n} P(w_{t+2}^j|w_1^{t+1})h(w_{t+1}|w_1^t) + \sum_{w_{t+1}^j\in\mathcal{W}^n} P(w_{t+1}|w_1^t)h(w_{t+2}^j|w_1^{t+1}) \\ &= \sum_{w_{t+1}\in\mathcal{W}^1}\left(h(w_{t+1}|w_1^t)\sum_{w_{t+2}^j\in\mathcal{W}^{n-1}} P(w_{t+2}^j|w_1^{t+1})\right) + \sum_{w_{t+1}\in\mathcal{W}^1}\left(P(w_{t+1}|w_1^t)\sum_{w_{t+2}^j\in\mathcal{W}^{n-1}} h(w_{t+2}^j|w_1^{t+1})\right) \\ &= \sum_{w_{t+1}\in\mathcal{W}^1} h(w_{t+1}|w_1^t) + \sum_{w_{t+1}\in\mathcal{W}^1} P(w_{t+1}|w_1^t)H_{n-1}(t+1) \\ &= H_1(t) + E(H_{n-1}(t+1)). \end{aligned}$$

Author Index